disrupting homelessness

OTHER TITLES IN

PRISMS

disrupting homelessness

Alternative Christian Approaches

Laura Stivers

Fortress Press / Minneapolis

To my daughters, Marijke and Annelies.
May they support hospitality, compassion, and justice and
be at home in God's inclusive community.

DISRUPTING HOMELESSNESS
Alternative Christian Approaches

Copyright © 2011 Fortress Press. All rights reserved. Except for brief quotations in critical articles or reviews, no part of this book may be reproduced in any manner without prior written permission from the publisher. Visit http://www.augsburgfortress.org/copyrights/ or write to Permissions, Augsburg Fortress, Box 1209, Minneapolis, MN 55440.

Scripture quotations from the New Revised Standard Version of the Bible are copyright © 1989 by the Division of Christian Education of the National Council of Churches of Christ in the United States of America and are used by permission.

Cover image: Tory Herman
Cover design: Laurie Ingram
Book design: Zan Ceeley, Trio Bookworks

Library of Congress Cataloging-in-Publication data
Stivers, Laura A.
 Disrupting homelessness : alternative christian approaches / Laura Stivers.
     p. cm.
 Includes bibliographical references and index.
 ISBN 978-0-8006-9797-6 (alk. paper)
 1. Church work with the homeless. 2. Church and social problems. I. Title.
 BV4456.S75 2011
 261.8'325—dc22

                           2010049014

The paper used in this publication meets the minimum requirements for American National Standard for Information Sciences—Permanence of Paper for Printed Library Materials, ANSI Z329.48–1984.

Manufactured in the U.S.A.
 14   13   12   11   1   2   3   4   5   6   7   8   9   10

Contents

Acknowledgments

My work has not been done alone, but in community. I thank the participants of the Presbyterian Taskforce on Homelessness for igniting my interest in the topic of homelessness and helping me to understand the complexities of addressing both homelessness and affordable housing. I would not have been able to write this book if not for the numerous people who were willing to share their perspectives and stories with me, from homeless people on the street, to families in transitional shelters, to the many people who work with the homeless and who work to provide affordable housing. While all of the insights I gained were invaluable for shaping my perspective, I, of course, am responsible for the ideas in this book.

Several forms of institutional and family support helped me to do this work. A Title III research grant through Pfeiffer University and an American Academy of Religion research grant helped fund my travel expenses for the interviews I conducted in three parts of the country (East Coast, West Coast, and the Midwest). Pfeiffer also gave me a semester sabbatical from teaching that gave me the luxury to write. A Pfeiffer student, Jonathan Smith, assisted me with a portion of the interviews. A colleague, Jennifer Ayers, graciously offered her home and car for me to do several of my interviews. My mom and stepdad, Sylvia and Ken Gentili, gave me a home with a beautiful view of the Puget Sound to spend sabbatical and, along with my dad and stepmom, Robert Stivers and Lora Gross, spent numerous hours playing with my children so that I could focus on my work. My daughters, Marijke and Annelies Pieters-Kwiers, offer me inspiration for making this world a more just and compassionate place for all.

Last of all, I am thankful for the many colleagues who encouraged me to turn my conference paper into a book (including Traci West, whose ethical method I used) and who then took my work seriously enough to read it critically and be in conversation with me. Colleagues from various social locations, Christian social ethicists, church leaders, social justice activists, housing policy experts, and homeless advocates have helped refine my ideas. Thank you especially to Robert Stivers, Rebecca Todd Peters, Gloria Albrecht, Elizabeth Hinson-Hasty, Monté Sorrells, Mark Stivers, Eileen Raphael, and Art Mielke. Michael West and Marissa Wold also deserve recognition for their guidance and direction in getting my ideas into print. Together we can all work in solidarity to bring about a more just and compassionate society where all people have a home in God's community!

Introduction

Is not this the fast that I choose:
    to loose the bonds of injustice,
    to undo the thongs of the yoke,
to let the oppressed go free,
    and to break every yoke?
Is it not to share your bread with the hungry,
    and bring the homeless poor into your house;
when you see the naked, to cover them,
    and not to hide yourself from your own kin?

Then your light shall break forth like the dawn,
    and your healing shall spring up quickly;
your vindicator shall go before you,
    the glory of the Lord shall be your rear guard.
Then you shall call, and the Lord will answer;
    you shall cry for help, and he will say, Here I am.
              —Isaiah 58:6-9

Daily newspaper headlines highlight a crisis of homelessness and affordable housing. Some allude to people trying to find a place to sleep: "Cities Deal With a Surge in Shantytowns"; "As Jobs Vanish, Motel Rooms Become Home"; "Sacramento and Its Riverside Tent City."[1] Others detail the mass of vacant homes resulting from the foreclosure crisis: "All Boarded Up"; "Painting Lawns Green."[2] One writer, commenting on the homelessness situation in Sacramento, suggests,

It seems that the city/county/state should at least be considering putting the homeless in the people-less homes and apartments that plague the area, rather than making permanent these squalid tent cities. They can probably acquire foreclosed homes for very little money and turn them into low-cost, affordable housing.[3]

The mayor of Sacramento responded that the city cannot acquire private property and that low-income housing stock is "maxed out, fully occupied."

Clearly, the economic crisis that began in 2008 has increased the number of people who are homeless. Multiple economic and social factors have precipitated a steady decline over the last thirty years in the standard of living of poor and working-class people (and even a substantial number of middle-class people). The proverbial American Dream is out of reach for increasing numbers of Americans as job security has become more tenuous, pay and benefits have decreased, and costs of basic goods like housing and healthcare have risen exponentially. While not all people end up homeless, many are a paycheck away from ending up on their friends' or families' couches.

Many Christians and church communities take Isaiah's call to house the homeless seriously. Some are involved in acts of mercy and compassion by providing financial support to groups who minister to people in poverty, and others are directly involved in addressing issues of homelessness and housing, either by volunteering at a shelter or soup kitchen and/or by participating on "builds" or other ventures to provide affordable housing.[4] While most Christians find such actions "Christlike," there is rarely any reflection on whether such actions are empowering for the people whom the volunteers are helping. This book aims to examine whether typical Christian responses to homelessness and provision of low-income housing are empowering for those who are being offered help and hospitality. It also seeks to broaden our responses to include changing structures and systems that cause poverty and brokenness in addition to responding with private charity.

A large part of the book deconstructs how our traditional Christian institutional responses often reinforce dominant ideologies about homelessness and housing in ways that both can be oppressive for those who are poor and/or homeless and can serve to mask the real causes of homelessness, thereby ensuring that the status quo of power and privilege remains intact. Christian churches in the United States typically respond to issues of homelessness and housing in two distinct ways: (1) a direct-service approach of providing shelters, food, and services, and (2) a more structural approach of building low-income housing. To analyze these types of approaches, I use two Christian institutions as case studies: the Association of Gospel Rescue Missions (AGRM), as a direct-service approach, and Habitat for Humanity International, as a provider of low-income housing. The latter part of the book analyzes the strengths and weaknesses of these approaches and then outlines an alternative approach of prophetic disruption that focuses on how individual Christians and church communities can respond to the problems of homelessness and housing in ways that challenge poverty and inequality in our society and offer structural solutions for preventing homelessness and substandard housing.

To aid me in both the deconstructive and constructive tasks, I will employ a liberationist ethical method, using the work of Christian ethicist Traci West.[5] Liberation theology and ethics began in the late 1960s and early 1970s in Latin America in response to traditional theological interpretations that focused on otherworldly salvation from God with no connection to the real material deprivation a majority of Latin Americans were suffering. Traditional theological interpretations served to justify the extreme wealth and privilege of a few as well as the immense landholdings of the Catholic Church in Latin America. Latin American liberation theologians and ethicists emphasized a God of liberation, using as exemplars of God's saving activity in this world Moses, leading the people of Israel out of slavery and Jesus, challenging the purity codes that served to marginalize and exploit particular groups of people. Soon, Christian communities in other areas of the world developed their own distinctive liberation theologies. While liberation theologies have changed and developed over the years, the core insight remains that this world (not simply an otherworld) should reflect God's intent for just and compassionate community. Thus, discipleship entails working toward such a vision.

Structure of This Book

In chapter 1, I give an overview of my ethical method, drawing on the work of Traci West. West argues that our Christian calling includes confronting that which denies human well-being and community; thus she emphasizes resistance and disruption of injustice. She assumes that social injustice will always be present; therefore, one's calling as a Christian will always include attentive listening to stories of injustice, determining appropriate societal response, organizing methods for enacting these responses, and continually resisting sources of injustice.

If we are to disrupt injustices and prophetically promote justice, we must have a well-grounded historical and social analysis of homelessness and housing. Therefore, an overview of our society's historical response to homelessness and housing and an explanation of dominant ideologies that influence our response are important. Unless we are aware of how these ideologies function, we will unknowingly adopt them and usually end up supporting injustice rather than enacting prophetic change. In chapter 2, I briefly outline the history of homelessness and housing in the United States, examine who is homeless and housed, and explore the purported causes of homelessness. Then I explain the current picture of homelessness and identify the economic policies that make it difficult for low-income people to access adequate housing.

In chapter 3, I lay out some dominant ideologies that influence how we respond to homelessness and housing. Our society bases its thinking and much of its social policy on stereotypes and half-truths of who is homeless and the reasons for their homelessness. Furthermore, we have a history of treating the so-called deserving poor differently from the so-called undeserving poor. Last of all, we equate the American Dream with owning a home and have a vision of the ideal homeowner. Our ideologies lead us toward individualistic solutions that focus on transforming the poor, rather than structural solutions that challenge social domination and inequality in our nation.

In chapters 4 and 5, I examine two common Christian responses to homelessness. One is a charity approach of providing shelters, clothes, food, and services. Whether it be in the form of a food bank, winter-coat drive, soup kitchens, or shelters, direct-service approaches are popular with churches and religious organizations, as they are less likely to involve the church in politics and do not upset the status quo. Furthermore, they appeal to the Christian sense of love and hospitality in the face of suffering and need and allow people to get involved directly with those who are in need.

The other Christian response is a more structural approach of building low-income housing. Many Christians realize that no matter how much charity they offer in response to homelessness, many people simply cannot afford a secure place to live. Generally, volunteers from churches do not have the time or the expertise to build affordable safe homes, but in coalition with other churches and nonprofits, it can be done. There are many forms this approach can take, from providing low-cost rental housing to helping people own homes.

To be able to do a more in-depth examination of common themes and ideologies in these types of approaches, I will highlight two organizations as case studies. I pick these organizations in particular because I think they exemplify typical Christian approaches to homelessness, and they are organizations with which many churches are involved. My work is not meant to be simply an examination of these two institutions, however. Instead, I am interested in how religious response in general reflects dominant American ideologies on homelessness and housing or prophetically disrupts such ideologies.

In chapter 4, I look at one example of a charity approach that offers shelters and services, namely the Association of Gospel Rescue Missions (AGRM). Based on literature from AGRM, observation of their practices, and interviews with both staff and clients, I examine key themes or beliefs that emerge. One belief is that homelessness is the result of individual behavior. Another is that homelessness is primarily a spiritual problem, not an economic issue. Still another theme is that the homeless need a work ethic and discipline to avoid dependency.

In chapter 5, I examine an organization that adopts a more structural approach of building low-income housing, namely Habitat for Humanity International. Based on literature from Habitat for Humanity books written by executive directors and others, observation of their practices, and interviews with both staff and clients, I focus on Habitat for Humanity's rationale for emphasizing homeownership, among various options, to address poverty. Furthermore, I examine how this emphasis shapes its practices and beliefs, specifically its views on volunteers and homeowners, its emphasis on sweat-equity hours, and its uplifting of private over public housing.

In chapter 6, I assess both the charitable and structural Christian responses to homelessness and housing. In particular, I look at the ways that each reflects the dominant ideologies of homelessness and housing, as well as the ways in which each has liberating aspects. I then examine how appropriating dominant ideologies undercuts the response, making it more difficult to promote a just and compassionate community where all are housed both physically and spiritually. From this assessment, I begin to outline how an approach of prophetic disruption might look different.

In chapter 7, I propose a theological foundation and rationale for why individual Christians and Christian communities should be part of a prophetic social movement to end poverty and homelessness. I conclude with a discussion of strategies that congregations and religious organizations have adopted to promote a home for all in God's just and compassionate community.

Solidarity with the Homeless

A goal of my teaching, writing, mentoring, and advocacy work has been, as Christian ethicist Traci West so aptly puts it, to build "just and compassionate relationships within and across our differing communities."[1] Discerning how to address adequately the problem of homelessness requires more than simply applying the Christian norms of hospitality or love of neighbor. Too often, our charity functions to make us feel good about ourselves, masking the need to see and respond to societal oppression. We can also become so caught up in our own understanding of what is liberating for others that we do not critically assess whether our assumptions and strategies truly lead to empowerment. We rarely give those who are recipients of our charity a defining voice in the process. Instead, we often blame the victims of societal oppression and poverty for causing the problems and further compound their victimization with our attitudes toward them and our solutions for solving "their" problems.

Such disempowering attitudes and actions led West to develop what she calls Christian "resistance" or "disruptive" ethics. *Resistance* and *disruption* refer to our Christian calling to confront, just as Jesus did, that which denies human well-being and community. For as long as humans have been around, domination and oppression have been used to gain power and privilege, and Scripture and theological rationales have been used to justify the status quo of inequality. Her method is similar to other liberationist ethics that refuse to appropriate Scripture, theology, and the Christian tradition in support of domination, but instead interpret Christian resources in liberating ways that support justice and compassion.

The concepts of resistance and disruption are especially useful for a study on homelessness because so many of our Christian responses, while hospitable in intent, do not challenge institutional inequality and oppression. While Jesus exhibited compassion on an individual level, he also challenged oppressive structures and practices. For example, he defied cultural and religious purity rules that defined who was clean and unclean by associating with lepers, tax collectors, and women, all of whom were considered impure. He challenged the Roman Empire's charitable system, which served to keep the poor in place, by multiplying the five fish and two loaves of bread, opening God's banquet for all. And Jesus confronted the exploitative behavior of the moneychangers in front of the temple, a system that religious and political authorities systemically supported. All of these examples have in common a picture of Jesus who promoted compassion for the downtrodden by disrupting the structural and ideological systems that create and justify poverty and oppression.

The end goal is not disruption for disruption's sake, but communities that foster spiritual wholeness. Embracing a liberationist method will entail participating in a process of building just and compassionate societies while simultaneously resisting entrenched and reemerging sources of injustice. Satisfaction of spiritual needs is an entitlement of human personhood, as much so for persons who are homeless as for persons who are housed. Such needs include connection with community, meaning and purpose in life, affirmation of personhood, and appreciation of the intangible mystical wonders of being in nature and humanity.[2] A truly Christian response to homelessness, then, must affirm the needs of those who are homeless for community, connection, and meaning. A Christian response must also celebrate the agency and spiritual vitality that people exhibit in their embodied responses of resistance in the face of oppression. Finally, a Christian response to homelessness entails building just and compassionate societies in *solidarity with* the homeless and poor, not *on behalf of* the poor.

Although West does not address homelessness and housing in her work, her ethical method provides guidelines both for critically analyzing various approaches to social issues and for constructing a positive Christian response. First, placing subjugated lives and voices at the moral center helps keep us accountable to create ideologies, practices, and institutions that uplift those who are most marginalized and exploited. Second, her ethical method insists that critical analysis always include (1) deconstructing social ideologies that are created to justify oppression and violence; (2) examining intersecting forms of social domination and oppression; (3) identifying complex individual and institutional power relationships; and (4) paying attention to the ways in which people are both victimized and have agency.

Paying attention both to the victimization that people on the margins face as well as to their ability to resist injustice avoids two problematic responses to homelessness. One is a "blame-the-victim" response, which sees individual irresponsibility as the sole cause for homelessness, and the other is a "patronizing-compassion" response, which views people on the margins as simply subjects of sympathy who need a saintly rescuer. Using a liberationist method allows us to examine critically dominant views on homelessness and housing and will help us to envision how we might continually resist and disrupt injustice while we simultaneously support the creation of compassionate and just structures and policies.

Placing Subjugated Lives and Voices at the Moral Center

We cannot be in solidarity with people who are marginalized and/or oppressed unless we recognize their reality as occupying the moral center. In analyzing ethical issues, we must *start* with the reality of "everyday people" who are from "areas commonly identified as problem communities."[3] The beginning point for many ethicists is moral theory and the testimony of "experts" on an issue. Christian ethicists might look to Scripture, theology, and/or the Christian tradition first. If ethicists include the experiences of everyday people, they are often white people, usually men (and increasingly white women). The experience of people of color, especially women of color, is always seen as an "addition." The goal is not to "assign specific valorized moral qualities" to the subjugated but to gain knowledge of what is needed to resist the conditions of marginalization and dehumanization that the homeless and poor face.[4] The voices of people who are homeless may reflect internalized oppression and should be critically assessed, but clearly a process of empowerment will not occur unless their experiences inform the solutions.

The goal is not to denigrate information that experts and professionals can provide but, rather, to gain knowledge that only those who have had these embodied experiences can impart. Such knowledge gives crucial insights for more adequate responses, often correcting stereotypes and mistaken assumptions of sources deemed authoritative. The voices of the subjugated are usually not heard. Even when their voices are heard, if their stories contradict public understandings and "authoritative evidence," then often their perspectives and contributions are dismissed. More often than not, the homeless are not permitted to speak, or they lose their sense of self and consequently their voice through internalization of negative definitions of self projected onto them from external sources.[5]

In examining the issue of homelessness, the starting point and moral center would not be experiences of middle-class, white homeowners but the numerous people of low or no income who are without homes and cannot secure affordable rental housing. To get a fuller picture, we would want to listen not only to the stories and struggles of people who are repeatedly on the streets, but also to the stories of individuals and families who are episodically homeless, as well as all the people who scrape by to stay housed and are increasingly losing their homes or rentals to mortgage foreclosure and eviction. Without knowledge of how the experience of each of these groups is different, we will be likely to lump all people who are homeless or poor into one category and label them. Furthermore, citing broad universal norms like "self-sufficiency" and "hard work" or utilizing theories on the causes of homelessness without knowledge from those who experience homelessness will be more likely to exacerbate than to solve the problem. If we are serious about addressing the problems of homelessness and inadequate housing, we must start by listening to people who experience the problems we are trying to address. Being aware of the actual conditions that entrap socially marginalized people would allow us to craft social policy that has a chance of ensuring people are housed and actually promotes individual and community well-being.

While we should begin with particular stories of subjugation, simply reciting narratives is not sufficient. We must join practical realities with theory that can offer critical analyses of social policies and practices. While theory is important, simply relying on broad universal values and understandings apart from particular stories can mask realities of oppression and ignore questions about whose interests are served.[6] For example, a common solution to homelessness and poverty is the promotion of classes that teach particular job skills and work etiquette. However, telling women who are homeless with children under six years of age that they simply need to have a better work ethic ignores realities such as low wages for "unskilled" labor and the high cost of child care and does not get at the issue of who benefits from low wages.

Examining particular public "practices" can be a test for what "universal values" we actually promote in society. Ethicists often emphasize the value of agency—that people have the freedom to make rational decisions based on a variety of choices—but fail to examine whether our societal practices support agency. For example, our society's lack of public investment in providing affordable and safe child care for families shows we do not give much value to the agency of poor single mothers. If we really valued their agency, we would make sure that they have access to child care, health care, and a number of other basic goods. The validity of solutions to homelessness and poverty must be assessed by whether they actually support liberation in the lives of the people the solutions are meant to help.[7]

Unraveling Social Ideologies

An important first step in the process of envisioning prophetic Christian responses to homelessness and housing is to assess critically our social ideologies about who is homeless and housed and how these ideologies have influenced our societal responses. Looking at historical responses to homelessness in the United States, we can see the connection. For example, when the homeless person was the feared male hobo, response was punitive. When the image shifted to white families during the Depression (despite the existence of many homeless families of color and single people), more supports were put in place, including public housing. As public housing became equated with black gangs in the 1970s and 1980s, funding dried up. Clearly, our dominant ideological social constructions guide our institutional responses.

We must be especially attentive to the ways in which our constructed ideologies can justify oppression and violence. Thus, a key aspect of ethical method is to identify and critique social ideologies and cultural myths that serve to support oppressive and discriminatory practices. After gaining an understanding of the ways in which we have responded to homelessness and housing as a society based on dominant cultural ideologies, we must step back and examine the moral focus presented. In West's work on domestic abuse, she argues that researchers have spent enormous amounts of time asking the question, Why do women stay?, when they should be asking, Why don't men let them go?[8] Similarly, we should ask why our society has allowed, and in many ways structurally supported, poverty and homelessness instead of asking what people do to cause their homelessness. We should not become entrapped by the perspective we are trying to oppose, however. That is, we should not expend all our energy disproving assumptions about who is homeless, thus diverting our attention from the root causes of homelessness.

We must not simply identify cultural myths and stereotypes but also show how these ideological constructions are actualized through institutional responses and particular practices. Doing so requires paying special attention to the intersection of the ideological constructions of race, class, gender, and sexual orientation and how they are repeatedly used to deny human well-being and to break bonds of solidarity. Our practices are the real test of our ethical commitments.[9] Thus, in examining Christian approaches to homelessness, attention to theoretical constructs as well as to actual practices will be important. Christian communities can often, consciously and unconsciously, uplift norms of human dignity, love, and solidarity, while simultaneously supporting discrimination and oppression.

Examining Power, Privilege, and Social Domination

Even if we are committed to placing socially marginalized lives at the center of our moral deliberation, our efforts can fail if we deny "the significance of how social domination confers entitlement, power, and status and identifies certain people as undeserving of equal treatment."[10] It is too easy for those of us with entitlement, power, and status to fail to see the privileges we have and to assume others have similar choices and agency. We rarely give thought to how we have benefited from historically oppressive policies and practices, nor do we ask many questions about whose interests are being served in current policies and practices. Many theological and philosophical ethicists do not make power analysis central to ethical method. Addressing the "role of racism or the historical biases and exclusions within European cultural systems" is optional in such approaches.[11] For an ethic to be liberating, it must include in-depth analysis of power relationships, both individual and institutional, with attention to historical foundations for current relationships of inequality and oppression.

Our racial, gender, and class identities shape how we are perceived and treated in society, yet many people believe that denying the significance of such identity factors, especially race, brings neutrality and therefore justice. For example, most institutions claim racial neutrality, while simultaneously supporting practices that reinforce white privilege.[12] Institutions also assume that most individuals will behave neutrally and not treat people based on race or class stereotypes. All of us are socialized into ways of thinking about the world that we believe to be neutral but are in fact influenced by dominant social ideologies that privilege white, male, heterosexual, and middle-class perspectives on the world. Thus, analysis of our individual and societal identities and worldviews for their oppressive elements is crucial if we are serious about justice. The mantra of neutrality is a convenient crutch for keeping unjust power relationships in place. Differences matter in a country and world with vast inequalities. We do not have a level playing field, and until we uplift those who are routinely disadvantaged by "neutral" attitudes and systems, we cannot equate neutrality with justice.

White churches have a history of paternalism founded on race-based understandings. To support liberation, individual Christians and church communities must first be cognizant of the varying degrees of power and privilege that particular individuals or groups of people have in any social situation; and, second, recognize individual and institutional practices of social domination based on race, class, gender, and sexual orientation. In short, we should assume that inequalities of power are central to any issue and always be ready to identify and resist the many ways that such inequalities are enacted and justified.

Even when we consistently recognize the interrelationship of all types of oppression and make analyses of relationships of domination and subjugation central, race routinely gets ignored or bracketed in ethical analysis. We do this either by ignoring the racial aspects of the story and focusing on the universal aspects or by seeing the story as only relevant to a particular racial group and not relevant to larger conversations in ethics. For example, in analyzing homelessness, we could argue that class oppression alone is a factor in who is homeless and simply ignore race oppression despite higher percentages of people of color in the ranks of the homeless. Or we could particularize the problem and chalk up the higher percentages to problems primarily within communities of color. Neither option identifies racism in our society as a problem.

One way we act in denial of power inequities is to assume that social problems like violence or homelessness are simply inevitable features of human society. Violence and injustice are not random or inexplicable phenomena. Any social repression can be historically traced, and for such repression to continue, it must be sanctioned and reinforced by humans, both individually and institutionally. For example, criminalizing and/or reforming those who are homeless are not new practices. We allow such practice because we can; people who are homeless have little political power.

Focusing on the moral failings of the victims of any social problem benefits those with power and privilege as it diverts attention from the inequitable institutions that are at the root of the problem. The way we justify repressive social policy that serves to buttress the status quo is to focus on the culture of the poor, that is, to show how poor people do not have middle-class values and then offer the paternalistic solution of teaching them to be "upright citizens." West's critique of shelters for battered women applies to homeless shelters as well. She argues that they focus on the "problems" of the women they treat (e.g., helping them overcome their "learned helplessness") without challenging forms of sexism and economic exploitation in society that support male violence. Similarly, in shelters and programs for the homeless, there is little focus on exploitation in society and lots on teaching "life skills" to people with so-called underclass values and practices. Such shelters "pose no real threat to the established arrangements of social power in the community."[13]

A dualistic perspective on power, in which we can clearly identify the "oppressors" and the "oppressed," is not helpful. All individuals occupy multiple roles and have multiple group identities that influence their behavior. While it is clear that more power is given to some social groups over others in our society, our mixed identities make power analysis complicated. The homeless have very little social power in our society, yet even among the homeless, people can inhabit roles of both oppressor and oppressed. For example, homeless women of color report that they often have little in common with white women, being routinely treated more negatively by the police, social workers, and the judicial system.[14] While white women might not always be aware of this differential treatment, they can unconsciously use it to their advantage in ways oppressive to women of color. A binary analysis of power can mask the destructive relationships that exist among racial, gender, or class groups. So while we need to be attentive to where the lion's share of power and privilege lies in society, such analysis does not discount the ways different types of oppression occur even among those who have little power and privilege.

False dichotomies can be misleading. We cannot assume, for example, that the theological stance of an individual or institution gives us a clear picture of their liberating potential. We should be open to the potential of many different perspectives (even apparently conservative ones) for liberation, and at the same time critically analyze all perspectives (even apparently liberal ones).

Identifying Victimization and Agency

While the homeless and poor have little political power, this does not mean they are simply victims without the ability to effect change (referred to as "agency"). In her work, West illustrates the multiple ways that black women are victimized but argues that focusing on victimization does not mean that black women who have suffered abuse have no agency. She refers to survivors of domestic abuse as "victim-survivors," noting that simply "when a woman survives, she accomplishes resistance."[15] In comparison, it will be important to recognize the multiple modes of resistance employed by the homeless without ignoring the realities of trauma and oppression they face.[16]

We must reject approaches that focus only on oppression. Such approaches can be used to support stereotypes and give credence to interpretations that suggest the pathologies of any particular group suffering from homelessness caused the problems; and they can keep us from recognizing and understanding resistance. However, the other extreme of focusing exclusively on the courageous responses people have in light of homelessness can negate the victimization they face.[17] We must take an integrated approach that does not overstate assertions of victimhood or of agency. On the one hand, we must resist labeling as pathological any group that experiences homelessness. On the other hand, analysis of the ways in which homelessness affects the psyches of people victimized is important. Ignoring the depression and self-doubt that homelessness can cause (normal reactions) is not liberating for people. Agency and victimization are not polar opposites. We must learn to recognize both in our analysis of homelessness. Paying attention to the ways that people who are homeless both negotiate their situation and resist it might dispel many of the myths and stereotypes that attribute their plight to laziness or lack of character. Such analysis might also give insight into the actual oppressive barriers that people face.

While some modes of resistance are healthier than others, we should be open to the possibility that all are "integral to making even the possibility of healing viable."[18] West cautions against identifying some forms of resistance as heroic and others as failures. She illustrates with an example of a girl who became a prostitute at age twelve to get away from an abuser. Rather than stigmatizing her behavior, we should acknowledge both her victimization and the steps she has taken to assert agency. Anger is another form of resistance that gets censured. Having a mind-set that all forms of resistance count can keep us from automatically labeling particular behaviors as pathological or destructive. Unless we can stand in the shoes of someone who is homeless and know the obstacles that person has faced in life, we cannot really know what counts as agency or passive acquiescence. Listening to a person's story and walking with someone in solidarity is the only way to gain insight.

Creating a Social Movement

Justice-making will always be a process, not ever a final achievement where we can rest easy. While we will always need to resist and disrupt forms of social domination, our final goal should be constructive. Thus, there must be a social movement that keeps the momentum of prophetic disruption going, that structurally addresses the root causes of poverty and homelessness and does not settle for short-term efforts at charity that do not address deep-seated domination and oppression. Although a social movement would challenge institutions that support oppression and encourage destructive ideologies, the goal is not to get caught up in ideological debates that entrap participants in conversations that distract from the ultimate goal of justice-making. A social movement should instead create public spaces for everyday people to participate in pluralistic dialogue about social values. A broad array of coalitions should be part of the dialogue and ensuing actions. The goal is not to create more bureaucracies where voices of opposition are subsumed (as always happens in bureaucracies) but to create a movement of coalitions that nurture prophetic disruption and the creation of a more just world.

A social movement will only be sustained by connecting politics and spirituality. Such a connection does not mean a deeper tie between church and state. Local church communities are important primarily because they have independence from both corporate and state control, giving them the ability to play an advocacy role. We can have an explicitly Christian approach to homelessness and housing and offer a moral voice in public dialogues, while also finding common values with non-Christians in constructing ethical responses. Politics occur "in the personal interactions between intimates as well as in public arenas like the mass media or a county domestic court system." Thus, strategic political connections are made in both the public and private realms of our lives.[19]

In a pluralistic social movement, different forms of spirituality will develop. These spiritualities will nourish and sustain a social movement, and provide a deeper moral basis and direction for the movement. Critical analysis alone will not create a "heightened moral sensibility." The movement requires "poetic work" that incites "dreams, passions, images," and contemplation about the dignity and well-being of the exploited and marginalized. In homeless newspapers and Internet sites, the homeless, through their art and poetry, offer spiritual foundations for the movement.[20] Claire J. Baker, a homeless poet, shares her poem "Truce on War" in the San Francisco Bay Area's homeless newspaper *Street Spirit*:

> You speak from
> that side of your mouth—
> I from this.
> Maybe someday we'll meet
> in the middle
> and share a kiss.[21]

Churches will ideally offer the critical analysis as well as the poetic imaging supportive of a movement for social justice.

The primary task of Christian faith communities is "truth work," that is, embodying the ways of Jesus and speaking truth against death-dealing realities. Churches are community organizations that can be involved in societal transformation, both by enacting the process of justice-making in their own communities and by joining the coalition of organizations that support a social movement of creating just and compassionate societies. To be involved in truth work today requires a shift in consciousness, moving from a "consumer/client" notion of citizenship that buys into the commodification of everything (including church affiliation) to a more participatory citizenship that embraces communal resistance and solidarity.[22] In other words, we can choose to make a right relationship with God, self, and others central, rather than buying into the image of ourselves as primarily consumers of the latest marketed ideas.

Churches must start with self-critique, eliminating any ideologies and practices that deny the spiritual and physical well-being of particular groups of people. Churches should also create resistance rituals, justice education that begins at a young age, and space for communal and peer sharing of resources to develop church responses to particular social issues. Finally, churches should participate in strategic conversations and actions that promote practices and policies for the well-being and dignity of those who are most marginalized and/or exploited, both in their own communities and beyond.[23]

Liberating responses will have to confront inequality and poverty, not simply by taking an oppositional stance to dominant culture, but through strategic resistance. No one-shot response will suffice. Only a social movement in solidarity with those who experience poverty will do. Such a movement will not simply address housing policy but will also prophetically address all social and economic policies that create poverty and vast inequality. An approach of prophetic disruption is less about reaching some ultimate finite goal than about participating in the hopeful process of becoming a more just and compassionate society. Such a process will always be a "perpetually unfinished task." Therefore, courage, vigilance, and deep spiritual resources will be necessary to uphold such an approach.[24]

Discussion Questions

1. What is your experience with homelessness and/or people who have been homeless? Are you familiar with responses that "blame the victim" or that offer "patronizing compassion"? How might a liberationist approach both disrupt poverty and oppression as well as create communities that foster physical and spiritual wholeness?

2. What would it mean to place subjugated lives and voices at the moral center when it comes to homelessness? How do we step out of our own worldview and truly hear perspectives different from our own? By what criteria do we assess different perspectives?

3. What would it mean to make power analysis central to the issue of homelessness and housing? How are power, privilege, and social domination connected to homelessness, and where do we see intersecting oppressions (e.g., race, gender, class) at work?

4. What is the importance of recognizing both victimization and individual agency in understanding homelessness? How do we avoid emphasizing one at the expense of the other?

5. What forms of Christian spirituality or "poetic work" can we draw on to nourish and sustain a social movement of justice-making? How do we encourage our faith communities to do "truth work," that is, confront inequality and poverty and support the dignity and well-being of all in God's creation?

−2−

Homelessness and Housing in the United States

Extreme poverty and homelessness are not as prevalent in the United States as they are in many poor countries. Nevertheless, an early morning ride on the metro system of any large city in the United States illustrates its existence. For example, one morning on Chicago's L route to O'Hare airport, each train car had at least three people (mostly African American men) carrying their worldly possessions in bags, trying to catch a few minutes of sleep before being forced to move to another train at the end of the line. They were not sleeping outside that morning because the temperature was ten below zero. These men on the L train are the visible homeless, but there are many invisible homeless, people who are sleeping in campgrounds, in cars, or at the homes of friends or family. Even for many who are housed, overcrowding or dilapidated dwellings can be a problem. There are, of course, different understandings of homelessness worldwide: "Residents of shantytown dwellings under a bridge or along a roadside are considered homeless in New York City, where such structures are not allowed, but are well-housed in many cities in the developing world, where such structures are the norm for millions."[1] While shantytowns have not been the norm for us in the United States, we are becoming accustomed to seeing tent cities in our midst.

As Christians, we ought to be outraged that anyone is homeless or lives in substandard housing when we consider the call from Isaiah and other prophets to God's justice of housing the homeless. While we are called to be disciples of peace and justice not simply within our own communities, in this book I will focus on the issue of homelessness and inadequate housing in the United States alone in order to influence individual Christians and church communities to think more deeply about how they approach the problem of homelessness in their immediate surroundings.

A key Christian mandate is to love one's neighbor, which entails offering hospitality to those who have less, often designated in Scripture as the alien, the orphan, and the widow. Many Christians and church communities do rise to the occasion when directly confronted with the plight of people in distress, as we saw in the way that Christian communities around the country responded with an outpouring of donations and volunteer aid after Hurricane Katrina. Church communities regularly donate food, money, and time to food banks and soup kitchens and often help build low-income homes through such programs as Habitat for Humanity.[2] Despite this outpouring of love and hospitality, most Christians are ignorant of the analyses of the causes of homelessness that have been done and the subsequent proposals to address the problem. Nor have they critically assessed the ways in which the homeless and the housed are portrayed in our society.

Without a critical analysis of housing and homelessness, individual Christians and church communities can often unwittingly reinforce some of the stigmas and structures that keep poverty and inequality in place. Furthermore, they can confine hospitality to charity and not envision avenues of advocacy for structural changes that might prevent homelessness.

Historical Snapshot of Homelessness and Housing

In the United States today, two-thirds of the population own a home, and most Americans think the federal government has some role to play in assisting people who are homeless. Both of these facts were new in the last century, however. In 1900, less than half of the population owned their homes,[3] and until New Deal federal legislation in the 1930s, local parishes, counties, or towns generally provided safety nets for people who were homeless. We went from an all-time low percentage of homeowners in 1940, of 44 percent, to a record high in 2004, of 69.2 percent, due to rising prosperity from development of the U.S. economy after World War II, as well as to multiple public policies that promoted homeownership, such as low-interest loans from Fannie Mae and savings and loans banks (the latter until the 1980s), the GI Bill, federal home mortgage insurance, and the home mortgage tax deduction.[4]

Homelessness in the United States has come in waves, but the consistent variable in each wave has been the health of the economy.[5] Although homelessness existed in the 1600s and 1700s, it was increasingly a problem in the United States in the early- to mid-1800s, as we transitioned to an industrial society with large numbers of people migrating to urban areas. At that time, the marketplace was flooded with cheaper goods, but there was more economic insecurity. African Americans, newly freed from slavery, disproportionately filled the ranks of the homeless. Big-city slums developed and philanthropists created private welfare institutions, with some cities providing shelter for the homeless in police stations.

From 1865 through 1880, the *images* of the "tramp" and "tramping" emerged. During the Civil War, men became accustomed to riding the railroad and engaging in small-group foraging expeditions for food supplements. Tramp colonies even mimicked army camp-life as a number of former soldiers participated in a life of tramping.[6] Rhetoric about the vagrant lifestyle was greater than reality, however. Fears in the 1870s fueled the trumped-up "tramp scare": "struggles between the propertied and unpropertied over the uses of public space, fears about the growth of a propertyless proletariat, and anxieties about the loss of traditional social controls in American cities."[7] Such rhetoric prompted a number of vagrancy laws and workhouse shelters. In reality, tramps were no different from the homeless since colonial times; they simply had greater mobility with the expansion of the railroad. Most were on the road due to "dislocation and unemployment or because of new opportunities resulting from economic expansion."[8]

While the recession of 1873 caused more homelessness, there was little public debate about alleviating it, as most people equated homelessness with a stereotypical image of the deviant, foreign-born, and lazy tramp. Reformers at the time did not connect the economic situation to increased tramping but instead focused on reforming immoral men through work.[9] Although homeless women existed during this time, they were made "invisible" by being placed in protective custody of charitable institutions or recruited into prostitution.[10]

As homelessness rates continued to increase into the early 1900s, the public's mood softened, and vagrancy laws were lightened in the North; yet the South continued to have strict vagrancy laws, even using chain gangs as punishment for vagrancy, to ensure a cheap labor force of African Americans.[11] Many communities offered a charity meal to people who were homeless but then sent them on to other communities. Large urban charities established shelters in the early 1900s, but they were not pleasant places to stay. Social reformers were heavily influenced by a new "scientific" view of homelessness, which claimed that indiscriminate giving promoted dependency and laziness and was more a cause of homelessness than unemployment. Thus, lodges that existed, such as those supported by the Charity Organization Society, required work for room and board, with the goal of inculcating industriousness over sloth.[12] Evangelical groups like the Salvation Army, who argued that all are worthy of Christ's love and salvation, introduced a competing perspective.[13] In fact, the gospel missions did not segregate and exclude blacks and other people of color until the 1920s.[14]

It was not until the Great Depression that homelessness was at the center of public debate and stereotypes lost their power in light of the real economic need of large numbers of people. Private volunteer organizations were not prepared to help these overwhelming populations. Consequently, shantytowns developed. No longer was the homeless person an "incorrigible tramp" but was instead one's neighbor or friend. With the Depression came the first federal program to address homelessness, the Federal Transient Service (FTS), part of New Deal legislation, which served to lighten the burden of local governments to care for the interstate transient populations. Through over three hundred transient centers in cities and three hundred camps in rural areas, the program assisted the transient male population.[15] Women were placed in boardinghouses rather than shelters and received more individualized attention from caseworkers.[16] The moralism and stereotypes of previous decades did not fully disappear, however, as the headline of the 1936 *Los Angeles Herald-Express* attests: "Urge Prison Camp Hard Labor for 'Box Car Tourists.'"[17] For a brief time, transient centers were created to help people with health care, meals, clothing, shelter, and job training as opposed to forced labor. These were closed in 1935, however, with the creation of Social Security and federal work projects.

The early 1900s saw the first appearance of "skid rows," a name originating from the "skid road" that lumberjacks in the Pacific Northwest used to transport logs and that later referred to the logging camps along the coast. Skid rows in the major cities clustered around the facilities created to aid homeless men. In the 1930s, these centers served as a place for men to find temporary work and a cheap place to live. Skid rows emptied out during World War I and especially World War II, when these men were seen as fit enough to be soldiers or to work in factories.[18] The few men that remained were older and too frail to work. Before the first World War skid-row exodus, there simply was not enough decent paying work for all men to afford housing.

When postwar economic expansion and the GI Bill helped many men, skid rows became even more stereotyped as dens of alcoholics who did not want to work. Skid-row men basically held three characteristics in common: homelessness, poverty, and personal problems. Many of them had made economic contributions as unskilled workers in agriculture, transportation, and construction industries, and some remained gainfully employed.[19] In many respects, they were not much different from the working class.[20] Single-room-occupancy hotels (SROs) and cage hotels[21] served as the primary housing for these men. Skid rows basically served as places to keep the "unwanted" of society segregated from the middle and upper class until the 1960s and 1970s, when cities underwent urban redevelopment and city planners, developers, and the media depicted skid rows as eyesores to be demolished.

Throughout the history of the United States, there have been groups of affluent persons who aimed to show that affordable housing could be achieved, but their projects never became large scale because affordable housing costs money. The government did not get involved in provision of affordable housing until Franklin Roosevelt's New Deal

legislation. The 1934 and 1937 National Housing Acts tied public housing to slum clearance,[22] with the creation of the first public housing built
by the Boston Housing Authority in 1935. In the 1930s and 1940s, most
major cities had projects to clear their slums and construct public housing. The rents for the better public housing (despite being subsidized)
were higher than the "slum" housing. Thus, the new tenants were better
off and basically displaced the previous residents of the neighborhood.

From the late 1930s through the mid-1950s, cities generally used
public housing to reward the "most meritorious of the working poor,"
not the unemployed, single parents, or nonwhite households.[23] Between
1949 and 1954, veterans and their families were the deserving recipients. Public housing at this point in history was seen as a privilege, not
a right.[24] Despite the construction of some 150,000 public housing units
by 1950,[25] the Federal Housing Administration (FHA), which had been
created in 1934, was much more influential in promoting homeownership with its FHA home mortgage insurance program[26] than it was in
providing low-income rental housing.

After World War II, a strong economy caused rapid urbanization
and suburbanization, especially of blacks migrating from the rural South
to the industrialized North. With this influx of low-income workers,
in addition to racial discrimination in housing and employment and
increasing urban disinvestment, "slums" reappeared. There were two
responses. One was President Truman's 1949 Housing Act, which made
"decent, safe, and sanitary" housing a national goal, creating a second
wave of public housing construction. The other response to burgeoning
slums was the Housing Act of 1954, which brought urban renewal (or
as others have negatively framed it, Negro removal).

Public housing was inhabited mainly by white nuclear households
at its inception, but with civil rights legislation, housing authorities
were pressured to house single-parent and nonwhite families. Public
housing quickly led to different demographics, as illustrated by Boston's
largest public-housing buildings, which were 80 percent white in 1964
and 70 percent black by 1970.[27] In 1969, Congress passed the Brooke
Amendment, limiting the amount of rent that tenants had to pay to
a percentage of their income (25 percent initially, and later raised to
30 percent).[28] As public housing increasingly housed a lower income

and racially diverse population (what many viewed as the "undeserving poor"), public sentiment turned against it.

Urban renewal had the worthy goal of revitalizing inner cities, but often entire neighborhoods were obliterated with the newly vacant land sold at low prices to private developers who did not construct low-income housing for the displaced residents of the area. Furthermore, new highways to connect growing suburbs to inner cities were built through the middle of many neighborhoods of color.

In 1965, the Public Housing Administration, the U.S. Housing Authority, and the House and Home Financing Agency all became part of the Department of Housing and Urban Development (HUD). Until 1987 and the Stewart B. McKinney Act (later named the McKinney-Vento Act), HUD had four core missions: to increase homeownership; assist low-income renters; improve the physical, social, and economic health of cities; and, after the Civil Rights Act of 1968, fight discrimination in housing markets. The McKinney-Vento Act added a fifth core mission of assisting homeless persons. In the 1960s and until 1973, HUD started fifteen new programs, its budget quadrupled, and its staff increased. In 1973, however, President Nixon halted any additional funding for programs and called for many programs to be restructured. Later, in the 1980s, President Reagan cut the HUD budget by more than half.[29]

Such budget cuts meant little funding was put toward upkeep of federal public housing units, and no new public housing units were built. In 1965, HUD had begun to lease privately owned housing to sublet to low-income families, which by 1974 transformed into the Section 8 certificate program, where families paid 25 percent of their income for rent and the government subsidized the remaining amount by paying the owners directly. The Section 8 rental voucher program began in 1984, whereby the fair market rent limitation was lifted and families had a predetermined calculation of assistance needs (which could be more or less than 30 percent). In 1998, Congress voted to merge the certificate and voucher programs into one Section 8 program, and families now have to pay at least 30 percent of their rent.[30] Funding for public housing and Section 8 has declined since its peak in 1978 despite growing need.[31] Now only one in four households that qualify for housing assistance receive it. Some cities have ten-year waiting lists for Section 8 vouchers,[32] and others have simply closed their waiting lists.[33]

The de facto rental housing creation program has been the Low Income Housing Tax Credit (LIHTC), which was created in the Tax Reform Act of 1986. The LIHTC is a tax credit to private investors who in return provide capital for affordable rental housing. Twenty percent of units must be rent restricted for occupants with 50 percent or less of area median gross income, or 40 percent of units for occupants with 60 percent or less of area median gross income. Five hundred thousand units were created from 1987 to 1994; however, the rent restrictions are required for only fifteen years, after which the rents can be raised to market level.[34]

While there have been no new public housing projects in years, Congress did pass legislation in 1992 creating HOPE VI grants for any public housing authority that has "severely distressed public housing." The grants assist in funding demolition of dilapidated public housing, development of mixed-income housing, and provision of supportive programs for residents, especially those relocated due to revitalization efforts. Purported goals of the program include changing the face of public housing and lessening concentrations of poverty.[35] Most low-income housing advocates agree with the goals of the program, but many have complained that not enough new affordable housing units have been created to relocate families from the demolished units, and thus many residents have not seen their situation improved.[36]

Housing assistance in our nation has overwhelmingly supported homeownership over rental assistance through tax deductions and credits. While not technically budget expenditures, the tax revenues not collected far exceed any amount of money spent on low-income housing assistance. According to the Center for Budget and Policy Priorities,

> When one hears the term "federal housing assistance," one typically thinks of the low-income housing programs operated by HUD. Yet the cost of these programs is dwarfed by the tax deductions and credits that the federal government provides each year to owners and builders of housing [namely the home mortgage interest deduction, the deduction for property taxes, the capital gains exclusion for home

sales, and the exclusion of net imputed rental income]. The four largest housing-related tax breaks for homeowners will cost $157 billion
in 2006, more than three times the total expenditures for all HUD
programs that year.[37]

Ironically, many experts argue that the home mortgage deduction does
not really increase homeownership. Over two-thirds of all taxpayers
do not itemize their deductions, and so the mortgage deduction does
not help them. Only half of all homeowners claim the deduction, and
half of the benefit goes to just 12 percent of taxpayers, with incomes
of $100,000 or more. While very little money is going to low-income
rental assistance, taxpayers can deduct up to a total of $1 million on two
homes, and up to $100,000 on a home-equity loan.[38]

Current Understandings and Demographics of Homelessness

Among homelessness experts there is a debate between two different
ways of conceptualizing homelessness. Such conceptual distinctions
matter for public policy, especially for determining who receives services. For example, HUD focuses on people who are literally homeless:

1. An individual who lacks a fixed, regular, and adequate nighttime
    residence; and
2. An individual who has a primary nighttime residence that is:
    a. a supervised publicly or privately operated shelter designed
        to provide temporary living accommodations (including
        welfare hotels, congregate shelters, and transitional housing
        for the mentally ill);
    b. an institution that provides a temporary residence for
        individuals intended to be institutionalized; or
    c. a public or private place not designed for, or ordinarily used
        as, a regular sleeping accommodation for human beings.[39]

Such a conceptual definition allows for easy measurement and clear
ability to track the effectiveness of programs.

An alternative definition is used by the Department of Education. It expands inclusion to children and youth who are "sharing the housing of others due to loss of housing, economic hardship, or a similar reason" as well as children and youth who "are living in motels, hotels, trailer parks, or camping grounds due to the lack of alternative adequate accommodations."[40] For example, in the 2006–7 school year, the Department of Education categorized 688,174 children as homeless, but only 32 percent of these children lived in shelters or outdoors. They did not meet HUD's criteria for homelessness and therefore were ineligible to receive emergency shelter or priority on waiting lists for public or subsidized housing.[41]

An expanded definition of homelessness would remedy such a problem.[42] Critics of an expanded definition claim it is too loose, with no clear methodology for identifying the population of hidden homeless. Furthermore, expanding eligibility for limited funding only fragments the services that are already being offered through HUD.[43] The National Alliance to End Homelessness claims that expanding the definition to include people who are doubled up for economic reasons would increase the homeless population fivefold[44] in a time when current homeless assistance grants fund shelters for only 56 percent of those who are defined as homeless by the narrower definition.[45]

Counting how many people are homeless is a difficult task, especially if the figures are to include people who are not literally homeless. HUD does a "point-in-count" estimate of people who are homeless in a single night in January, but there are far more people who are homeless over the course of a year. In January 2009, the number was 643,067, with 63 percent of those persons sheltered and 37 percent unsheltered.[46] Since the HUD numbers are limited to people in shelters or on the street, these findings do not include the hidden homeless and therefore underestimate the number of people who are homeless. The National Coalition for the Homeless notes that many cities turn people away from shelters for lack of room, and there are few or no shelters in rural areas, where about 9 percent of the nation's homeless reside. Basic consensus among organizations focusing on homelessness is that there are approximately 3.5 million people who experience homelessness in a given year, with 1.35 million of them children. This translates to 1 percent of the U.S. population experiencing homelessness each year, with almost 40 percent of that number being children.[47]

The population of homeless is quite diverse, with the only consistent common denominator being extreme poverty. Since 1984, researchers have classified people who are homeless into three groups (although the groupings are not always distinct): first-time/crisis/transitional, episodic, and chronic.[48] *Transitional homelessness* refers to individuals or families who are homeless only once or twice and for a short period of time, usually related to an unexpected crisis such as unemployment, divorce, or eviction. *Episodic homelessness* entails people who cycle in and out of homelessness for differing lengths of time, often related to inpatient treatment centers, detoxification programs, or jail. *Chronic homelessness* includes people who have lived on the streets or in shelters for prolonged periods of time and who usually face many obstacles to holding secure employment or housing.[49]

The question of what percentage of the homeless population each group represents is difficult to answer because it depends in part on the way researchers are defining the categories, where they are sampling people (e.g., in shelters or more broadly), and the state of the economy at the time of the study. A dated study by Martha Burt and her colleagues from the Urban Institute (1996) reported 20 percent in the crisis group, 24 percent in the episodic group, and 56 percent in the chronic group.[50] Based on HUD's 2007 point-in-count data, the National Alliance to End Homelessness claims that only 18 percent are chronically homeless.[51] The Burt study was conducted over three months, while the HUD data is from their annual single-night census. The HUD data does not include people in the crisis or episodic group. Furthermore, all of these statistics are based on an understanding of literal homelessness; they do not include the hidden homeless, people doubling up with family or friends, people staying in motels or campgrounds, or people in shelters for domestic violence. Researchers who include hidden homelessness would presumably show a much lower percentage of people who are chronically homeless and a higher percentage in the crisis group.

Although the only consistent variable for people who are homeless is extreme poverty,[52] there are some characteristics that are found in higher numbers among people who are homeless versus people who are housed. Noting such characteristics does not imply causality, however. Of the single homeless population, 67.5 percent are male, but of the homeless families with children, 65 percent are households headed by a female.[53] Although ethnic and racial makeup varies by region, the racial statistics of the homeless population are 47 percent African American, 47 percent European American, 4 percent Native American, and 2 percent Asian American. By ethnicity, 24 percent of the homeless population is Hispanic American.[54] Up to one-fourth of the urban homeless population are employed.[55]

Veterans make up 20 percent of people who are homeless.[56] About half of the people experiencing homelessness suffer from mental-health issues, with one-fourth having a serious mental illness.[57] According to the Federal Task Force on Homelessness and Severe Mental Illness, only 5 to 7 percent of homeless people with mental illness require institutionalization, however.[58]

Families with children are the fastest-growing segment of the homeless population. The U.S. Conference of Mayors 2007 survey estimates families with children to be 23 percent of the homeless population, with one-third of the parents working.[59] Single women who have very young children and limited education head most of these families.[60] Anywhere from 15 to 50 percent of female-headed households experience homelessness due to domestic violence.[61]

Age is also a factor. While the full extent of youth homelessness is unknown, around fifty thousand youth are on the streets for six months or more.[62] In 2004, 25 percent of the homeless were ages twenty-five to thirty-four, whereas only 6 percent were ages fifty-five to sixty-four.[63] As many as 25 percent of those who experience homelessness have spent time in foster care or other placements (compared to 3.4 percent of all American adults).[64]

One of the most prevalent characteristics that people associate with homelessness is addiction disorders. Some studies have found rates as high as 65 percent, but the National Coalition for the Homeless argues that this figure is misleading:

The 2007 United States Conference of Mayors "Hunger and Homelessness Survey" reports that approximately 9.6% of the homeless population in a family with children is dealing with issues of substance abuse while 37.1% of homeless individuals are dealing with these issues. Studies that report substantially higher numbers often over-represent long-term shelter users and single men, and use lifetime rather than current measures of addiction. Another important aspect to consider is that many addiction issues arise while people are experiencing homelessness, rather than causing them to become homeless.[65]

Researchers at the Urban Institute argue that at any given time, half the people who are homeless have had problems with alcohol in their lives, and one-third with drugs, but note that not everyone who has had a problem still has one. They argue that the connection of addictions and homelessness is exaggerated, yet a factor nevertheless.[66]

Causes of Homelessness

Some experts on homelessness have used the analogy of musical chairs to illustrate the causes of homelessness:

> In the analogy, the players are poor households, and the chairs are the housing units they can afford; if there are fewer affordable units than poor households, some will be left homeless when the music stops. The children who fail to nab chairs are those who move more slowly than others. Similarly, individuals and families who fail to obtain housing, under conditions of scarcity, are those who are most vulnerable, by reason of individual factors or social exclusion. However, the level of scarcity is a joint function of housing supply, prices, and subsidies; incomes at the bottom of the distribution; and social welfare spending.[67]

Clearly, poverty is a key cause of homelessness in our country. Poverty has increased in the last thirty years due to eroding wages and benefits for work, as well as the declining value and availability of public assistance. In conjunction with a severe lack of affordable housing, more people have become homeless. Personal factors, such as addiction, disability, mental illness, or experiences with foster care, jail/prison, or domestic violence can also be contributing causes of homelessness, especially when it comes to who is most vulnerable in an inequitable society. Further, structural oppressions based on factors such as race, gender, class, sexual orientation, and disability contribute to vulnerability in a competitive economy. Martha Burt and her colleagues at the Urban Institute explain the connection of both structural and individual factors:

> Over the years, most people have come to recognize that both structural and individual factors play a role in producing homelessness. The structural factors set the stage, without which fewer people would be homeless. They help to answer the question, "Why more homelessness *now*?" . . . Then the individual factors help to identify "*Who?*"—which particular people subject to the worst combinations of structural factors are most likely to lose their housing. However, as the structural conditions worsen, even people without personal vulnerabilities other than poverty may experience crises that precipitate a homeless episode.[68]

Finally, the existence of a sufficient safety net in society plays a role in whether structural or individual factors will cause homelessness.

When a sample of homeless people was asked about the source of their problems, 94 percent said, "No place to live indoors," and 88 percent said, "No money." No other answer was shared by more than half the sample.[69] In the last thirty years, wages (adjusted for inflation) have gone down for 80 percent of workers in the United States. In addition, job security has been steadily dismantled. When U.S. postwar hegemony diminished, corporations found they could not make the same profits (or any profits at all) from production, and so well-paying manufacturing jobs decreased. Many of these jobs went overseas as corporations could find a cheaper labor supply and less restrictive labor and environmental regulations in developing countries. A number of corporations got involved in mergers and acquisitions to make higher profits, contributing to more job loss.[70] There was basically a shift from investment in production to investment in finance as a source of profits. Financial maneuverings were increasingly unregulated, which led to dubious investments and financial speculation, such as subprime mortgage securities, excessive leveraging of stocks, and derivative securities.[71]

A core-periphery system developed, where the profit-making core workers continued to do well, with large salary increases, and the peripheral workers were increasingly disposable, with declining wages and benefits. Furthermore, competition from the global economy as well as antilabor governmental policy led to the weakening and decline of labor unions and consequent worker disempowerment. The development of corporate models like that of Walmart, where a large economy of scale with the ability to force suppliers to cut prices has combined with sophisticated antiunion strategies, has also led to declining wages and benefits for many.[72] While wages have gone down and benefits have been cut or decreased for most Americans, many household costs have increased, most notably health care. In 2009, over fifty million Americans (19 percent of population under sixty-five) were without health insurance,[73] and rising health-care costs have routinely outpaced inflation each year.

For individuals (especially single parents with small children) who have barriers to employment, the availability of public assistance has decreased in the last ten years. The Personal Responsibility and Work Opportunity Reconciliation Act of 1996 (PRWORA), more commonly known as welfare reform, was touted as a way to encourage work and discourage dependency, but after a decade, most low-income families are not doing better. Aid to Families with Dependent Children (AFDC), which was formerly an entitlement for individuals and families with sufficient need, was switched to Temporary Assistance to Needy Families (TANF) and now includes time limits, work requirements, and sometimes stricter eligibility requirements if the block-grant funding from the federal government runs out.

Some politicians touted welfare reform's 50-percent caseload reduction as a success, but long-term studies have shown that although more former welfare recipients are employed, their incomes are very low ($7–8 per hour, minimal benefits). A substantial number of poor single mothers are now both jobless and do not receive cash assistance, affecting roughly two million children. Although child poverty fell during the 1990s (during a strong economy), between 2000 and 2004 children living in families with cash incomes below half the poverty line increased by 774,000. While this increasing poverty could be due to a number of factors, fewer children now get assistance from TANF. In the early 1990s, 80 percent of families who were poor enough to qualify received assistance (formerly AFDC); by 2002, only 48 percent of families received TANF assistance. PRWORA cut $55 billion in other low-income programs as well, half of that reduction made in the Food Stamp Program and the rest by restricting eligibility for legal immigrants to Supplemental Security Income (SSI), food stamps, and Medicaid, and for some children with disabilities to SSI.[74] A more recent development is cash-strapped states eliminating General Assistance (GA), a support of last resort for individuals who are not eligible for other forms of assistance. GA is especially important for single people who do not qualify for assistance reserved for families.

A race and gender analysis of both lowering wages and weakening public assistance helps explain some of the evident disparities of homelessness. Single mothers with children under the age of six cannot afford child care on low-wage jobs, yet only one out of ten children who is eligible for child-care assistance under federal law gets any help.[75] Almost 60 percent of minimum-wage workers are female, and 40 percent are people of color. Thus, the new increase in the minimum wage to $7.25 an hour certainly helps. (Without the increase, a single parent with two children was living substantially below the poverty line.)[76] Women of color are disproportionately the recipients of TANF (around 24 percent white, 43 percent black, 30 percent Hispanic).[77]

Although the income of low-income households is significantly below the median, the following statistics illustrate racial disparity. In 2009, median income for white households was $51,861, for Hispanic households $38,039, and for black households $32,584.[78] When wages decrease and public assistance is less readily available, it is low-income people of color and women with children who suffer disproportionately. Housing and job discrimination for people of color and women with children also has a negative effect. For example, an investigative study conducted by HUD in 2000 found that whites receive more favorable treatment than blacks in 21.6 percent of tests for rentals.[79] Another study found that mothers' wages were only 60 percent of fathers' wages, while the wages of young women without children were close to those of men.[80]

After World War II, there was plenty of affordable rental housing, as well as inexpensive single-room-occupancy (SRO) housing, but in the 1970s and 1980s much of the affordable rental housing became higher priced, and SROs were demolished as a part of urban renewal. Now there are 5.8 million more extremely low-income households than there are affordable housing units.[81] According to the Joint Center for Housing Studies, 39 million households paid more than 30 percent of income on housing (traditionally 30 percent has been considered "affordable"),[82] and almost 18 million paid more than 50 percent of their income on housing in 2007.[83] HUD estimates that the number of households experiencing "worst case housing needs"[84] increased by 23 percent between 1999 and 2005.[85] Low-income households suffer the biggest cost burden, with three-quarters of low-income households severely cost-burdened in 2007.[86] The national hourly wage needed to afford rental housing in 2009 was $17.84 (much higher than any state's minimum wage).[87] For most households, the problem is a severe rent burden, not inadequate housing.

Other factors that *can* contribute to homelessness are domestic violence, mental illness (including post-traumatic stress disorder for veterans), addiction disorders, reentry from prison, and youth exiting from foster care. None of these factors alone is usually the direct cause of homelessness, but each can contribute to an individual's inability to work and/or afford housing. Domestic violence is claimed to be one of the leading causes of homelessness for women and children. Sometimes domestic violence can be the direct cause of an episode of homelessness, especially if a woman and children are fleeing a situation of violence. Even if not directly the cause, trauma from violence is a factor in homelessness, as 92 percent of homeless women have experienced severe physical or sexual abuse at some point in their lives, and 63 percent have been victims of domestic violence as adults.[88]

There is clearly a correlation between mental illness and homelessness, yet it is debated whether the number of homeless people with mental illnesses is the direct result of the closing of mental institutions. Many of them were closed in the 1950s and '60s, whereas homelessness did not substantially increase until the 1980s, when competition for scarce low-income housing began.[89] Everyone agrees, however, that the intended network of community support services after deinstitutionalization, such as halfway houses, supported housing options, and community-based mental health centers, never did materialize to an adequate extent. Many researchers argue that people do not become homeless simply because they are mentally ill but rather because there is a lack of housing that meets their needs. In fact, homelessness itself might be the cause of some minor mental illnesses, such as anxiety or depression.[90]

While alcohol and drug abuse is higher among people who are homeless, the lack of affordable housing and not the abuse is the root cause of their homelessness. In the past, skid rows had SRO hotels and flophouses where people could sleep cheaply, and there were day-labor outlets where people could pick up temporary jobs. Both of these resources have all but disappeared, with SRO hotels demolished in urban renewal and day-labor outlets replaced by temp agencies like Manpower.[91] A compounding problem is the lack of treatment facilities for people of little or no means. The National Association of State Alcohol and Drug Abuse Directors says that only 50 percent of those who need treatment receive it.[92]

Every year, at least 650,000 people leave state and federal prisons, and even more leave local jails.[93] Many of these people rely on families for housing, but often they go back to communities with high poverty and a lack of jobs and affordable housing. Although there are no national statistics on prison reentry and homelessness, a California study estimated that 10 percent of parolees in the state are homeless, with 30 to 50 percent in large urban areas like San Francisco and Los Angeles.[94] Released prisoners have difficulty finding stable and adequate income. A record of incarceration can lead to stigmatization and discrimination and even to being banned from certain professions. The longer people stay in prison, the less likelihood they have of participating in the legitimate labor market. Obstacles to finding housing include lack of money for a security deposit along with reference and criminal background checks by landlords.[95] People of color are disproportionately affected because their incarceration rate is so much higher, in part due to racism in the criminal-justice system.[96]

Young people who have been in foster care can have a difficult time finding stable housing in young adulthood. For example, 25 percent of former foster youth claim to have been homeless at least one night within two-and-a-half to four years after exiting foster care.[97] These youth can lack the support networks that people rely on in crisis. Furthermore, foster care might not have helped children deal with problems that caused them to be put in foster care. Most people, however, who experience foster care do not become homeless as adults.[98]

Current Situation of Housing and Homelessness

Since the 1980s, the numbers of people who are homeless has steadily increased, except for a small decrease in the number of chronically homeless people between 2005 and 2007.[99] That decrease was a result of HUD's emphasis since 2001 on ending chronic homelessness.[100] One method for reaching this goal was and continues to be "Housing First," an approach to get people who are chronically homeless into supportive housing. The premise is housing first, then services. The rationale for focusing on those most in need is in part an economic one since people with chronic illnesses use many public systems in an inefficient and costly way (e.g., emergency rooms, corrections, mental health). Furthermore, 10 percent of the homeless population account for 50 percent of the shelter beds used annually.[101] Putting people who are chronically homeless in housing with support services is less costly than the inefficient alternatives. For example, Minnesota saved $9,600 per person in costs to the state through Housing First programs. In addition, employment there increased by 26 percent.[102] Housing people who are chronically homeless also frees up space in the shelters for others who are temporarily homeless.

Although funding for homelessness has been one of the few areas of social safety-net spending that has increased in recent years (mainly to address chronic homelessness through shelters and housing with services), there has been little funding for low-income rental assistance despite the increasing income/housing affordability gap.[103] The number of low-income families with housing affordability problems has increased by 33 percent since 2000 to nearly nine million in 2007.[104] Yet the nation has lost around 200,000 public housing units over the past decade (with only 50,000 being replaced) and 150,000 Section 8 vouchers between 2004 and 2007.[105] The continuing cuts in federal support for public housing and rental assistance and the conversion of subsidized private housing developments to market-rate housing when their contracts expire will only increase the number of people eligible for Section 8 vouchers. In light of the increase in federal budget deficits from tax cuts and massive defense spending since 2001, the large bailouts for banks and other industries in 2008–9, and lower federal tax revenue in this time of recession, cuts to low-income housing assistance are likely, only increasing the number of people who will experience homelessness.

The current foreclosure and economic crisis will increase the ranks of the homeless. By 2005, one in four home loans was subprime, which typically means higher interest rates that are adjustable and not fixed. African Americans were 450 percent more likely to receive a subprime loan than whites (even when they qualified for a loan at lower rates).[106] The numbers of foreclosures are staggering: "A record 2.8 million U.S. properties received foreclosure notices in 2009, up 21 percent from 2008 and up 120 percent from 2007."[107] With former homeowners turning to the rental market, affordable housing will become even more limited.[108]

In addition to losing their homes as well as any home equity, householders who are foreclosed on also deal with a ruined credit rating that can cause long-term financial difficulty. We typically imagine the victims of the foreclosure crisis as homeowners who cannot make their mortgage payments on time, but over 20 percent of foreclosed properties have been rentals, and around 40 percent of the families that face eviction due to the crisis are renters, with low-income families and minority communities hit the hardest.[109]

Increasingly, the face of homelessness is families with young children. For example, in New York City the number of homeless families with children hit a record high in November 2008, up 40 percent from the previous year.[110] More than one in six children live in households paying more than half their income for housing, making them more likely to live in crowded or inadequate conditions. Our current economic crisis and resulting job losses put these families at incredible risk of homelessness if there are no prevention programs. The Center for Budget and Policy Priorities notes that our safety net does less to protect against deep poverty than it did in the past, with 71 percent of people lifted out of deep poverty in 1995 versus only 56 percent in 2005.[111]

Conclusion

Homelessness is clearly linked to structural factors, namely a lack of affordable housing, poverty, and oppression. We have a political economy without enough jobs for everyone, and too many jobs with inadequate pay and benefits. Furthermore, since the 1980s we have a smaller safety net to catch those who fall through the cracks. The government has had programs aimed at addressing structural economic factors. In the past, it has funded public housing, and currently it offers rental assistance for low-income families. Yet, financial assistance, usually through tax breaks, has often promoted homeownership over rental assistance.

Individual factors also play a role in who ends up homeless. While extreme poverty is the only consistent commonality among people who are homeless, race and age are factors, with a higher percentage of people of color and young people experiencing homelessness. Veterans, people with mental illnesses, and people with addictions also represent a higher percentage of the homeless population. Increasingly, families with children are filling the ranks of the homeless. We are not always aware of the prevalence of homeless families, as they are more likely to be part of the hidden homeless, who are staying with family or friends or sleeping in cars or campgrounds. The chronically homeless are more visible, a population that is still predominantly male.

How can individual Christians and church communities be effectively involved in addressing the problem of homelessness? Do we leave responsibility for addressing structural causes to the government and focus more simply on providing direct hospitality in our communities? Do we get involved in community organizations that advocate for affordable rental housing or build low-income housing? Do we create social movements for broad economic change? Our responses will be influenced by what we see as the main causes of homelessness as well as what roles we think churches, community organizations, businesses, and government should have. Having some understanding of how we have responded to homelessness and housing in the past as well as a picture of the landscape today helps us to envision our own response.

Discussion Questions

1. How has your faith community offered love of neighbor to those in need? Have you ever given any critical thought to whether your community's hospitality has been empowering for the recipients or whether it prevents homelessness and poverty?

2. Does our history of the ways we have viewed the homeless and the ways we have addressed homelessness and housing inform your perspective in a new way?

3. Where did you get your understanding of the main causes of homelessness? Were any of your understandings challenged by information in this chapter?

4. Had you ever considered the diversity among people who are homeless? Were you aware of the hidden homeless or that many of the homeless are children? Does this information change your perspective?

5. The current recession and foreclosure crisis has increased the number of people who are homeless, the effects often reaching into middle-class congregations. What kind of responses do faith communities envision in light of the current landscape, and what has worked in the past?

-3-

Dominant Ideologies
on Housing and Homelessness

Mainstream American ethos has been built around the values of equality, success, and democracy. Many believe that in a democratic society with equal opportunity for all, people will be successful if they work hard enough. The assumption is that if there is equality and opportunity for democratic participation, people are responsible for their own socioeconomic fate. While substantial evidence shows that our society comes up short when it comes to equality and opportunities for democratic participation, public opinion has generally held that personal traits rather than structural factors explain success or failure.

In light of this individual focus and our belief in a meritocratic society, owning a home and property becomes a symbol of the American Dream—proof that one has worked hard, behaved respectably, and contributed to society. The flipside is that homelessness is equated with laziness, deviance, and lack of upright citizenship and contribution to society.

In this chapter, I will give an overview of some of these dominant American ideologies to set the stage for understanding how many Christian responses to homelessness often buy into the ideologies, albeit unconsciously, that may further exacerbate the problems they are trying to address. Most Americans are aware of poverty and the problem of homelessness in our country, and many have compassion and want to address the problem. Yet, despite our best intentions, ingrained

ideologies we have about both who is homeless and why they are homeless can result in actions and policies, often stemming from good intentions, that further stigmatize people and fail to address the problems of
poverty and homelessness.

Homeowners as Responsible and Autonomous Citizens

> To possess one's own home is the hope and ambition of almost every
> individual in our country, whether he [or she] lives in a hotel, apart-
> ment, or tenement. . . . Those immortal ballads, "Home Sweet Home,"
> "My Old Kentucky Home," and "The Little Gray Home in the West,"
> were not written about tenements or apartments. . . . They never sing
> songs about a pile of rent receipts.[1]

Since the 1930s, U.S. presidents have equated homeownership with
security, autonomy, and middle-class values. Herbert Hoover called
the owner-occupied home "a more wholesome, healthful, and happy
atmosphere in which to raise children." In the 1960s, Lyndon Johnson
declared that "owning a home can increase responsibility and stake out a
man's place in his community. . . . The man who owns a home has something to be proud of and reason to protect and preserve it." In the 1980s,
Ronald Reagan said that homeownership "supplies stability and root-
edness," and in the 1990s, Bill Clinton claimed that "more Americans
should own their own homes, for reasons that are economic and tan-
gible, and reasons that are emotional and intangible, but go to the heart
of what it means to harbor, to nourish, to expand the American Dream."[2]
    Sociologists, urban planners, and criminologists have all extolled
the benefits of homeownership: more stable neighborhoods and communities, increased financial security, generation of jobs, better care of
property, more civic involvement, and healthier children and families.[3]
Their studies have been used to support the idea that owning a home
symbolizes stability, accomplishment, respectability, relationships of
care, and hard work. The ideal of homeownership has a long history in
the United States, as seen in this 1922 *Own Your Own Home Resolution*
from a Boston newspaper's "book of homes" supplement:

I believe in the American home and its eternal power for good;
I believe that it is my individual duty and privilege to own a home
under the Stars and Stripes; I believe that Boston is one of the great
home cities of the world; I solemnly resolve to make my best efforts
during 1920 to become a homeowner in this great city [Boston], and
thereby satisfy the cravings of my own heart and the desire of those
dear to me in life; to make my own prosperity more secure, and also
to stimulate through home ownership the industrial and commercial
life of my own city.[4]

The National Association of Real Estate Boards noted in a 1922 book
that "Home Owning Breeds *Real* Men."[5] The Department of Housing
and Urban Development (HUD) even urges faith leaders to support
homeownership: "Faith leaders are influential voices in their communities. Be a trumpet for the wealth building, family nurturing and
community improving aspects of homeownership. Help your members see the possibility, overcome their apprehensions and realize their
dream."[6] The family and private household (homeowner household, of
course) are perceived as havens in a heartless world.[7] In sum, homeownership is connected with family values and the uplift of church
and state.

While homeownership *can* generate financial stability, strengthen
communities, and generate jobs, there is more rhetoric given to the
benefits of homeownership than actual empirical evidence. Political
scientist Kathleen Arnold writes,

Home is conceived of as a site unmarked by difference, tension, or
struggle. In contrast, homelessness represents the problems outside
of the home: the breakup of the nuclear family, mental illness, pro-
miscuity, and addiction. It is as if one group is problem free and moral
and the other epitomizes social problems and immorality.[8]

In the 1800s, the home became a site of virtue, nurture, and civilization
that women guarded and a refuge for men from the world of competitive work.[9] The rise of the homeless "tramp army" in the late 1800s was
seen as a "breakdown of domestic relations," with men severed from the

home and their breadwinning duties.[10] Similarly, in the postwar era of the 1950s, skid rows were seen as a "blatant affront to the nuclear family ideal," a threat to gender and family norms, and even national security itself.[11] In short, owning a home has been part of the American Dream and symbolizes freedom, security, mobility, and community.[12] Despite a lack of evidence, we equate the behavior of buying a home with a number of positive behaviors and values, and the behavior of losing a place to live with negative behaviors and values.[13]

The symbol of the home has also been associated with particular places. Originally, the home was associated with rural landscape and the small family farm (e.g., "home sweet home").[14] With the urbanization of America and resulting white flight to suburbs, the "respectable home" was situated next to similar homes with white picket fences, epitomized by 1950s television shows like *Leave It to Beaver*. Rural areas, and then particular suburban neighborhoods, were idealized as the space of home and community, as well as of safety from the perceived crime, dirt, and poverty of city spaces. The association of the home with pure rural/suburban areas has resulted in homelessness being viewed as a strictly urban problem, and the association of the rural/suburban home as privileged and pure has led to efforts at preservation and protection against perceived marginal groups of people (e.g., Not in My Backyard [NIMBY] campaigns against homeless shelters and low-income rental housing).[15]

While Americans have historically equated modest homes with accomplishment and hard work, increasingly, bigger and bigger homes are part of the American Dream. In 2004, real estate agency Coldwell Banker reported that its sales of U.S. luxury homes valued at $1 million or more hit an all-time high of $35.5 billion, surpassing its previous record of $23.3 billion, set in 2003.[16] As taxpayers, we support buying bigger by offering home mortgage interest deductions on up to two homes even though over 80 percent of these benefits go to households in the highest income quintile.[17] The justification for such tax breaks is stimulation of economic growth.

If the ideal American vision is communities of industrious, civic-minded homeowners, the good homeowner becomes the norm of respectability. The ideal image of the "good" homeowner is a heterosexual, middle-class nuclear family, with the assumption that such house-holds are healthy and thus the foundation for economic and political independence.[18] This homeowner image is popular in part because it connects to the rhetoric of "family values" promoted by the Christian Right. While not all people agree with the Christian Right and, empirically, American families are overwhelmingly more diverse than the vision of a patriarchal nuclear homeowner household, this vision has influenced American thinking nevertheless.

The idea of homeownership has a long history of being associated with responsibility and citizenship. For Aristotle, the household was the foundation of the state; thus, he understood homelessness to undermine civic duty and political identity.[19] Social-contract theorist John Locke laid the foundation for our images of citizenship when he argued that certain groups, such as unpaid workers (e.g., women) and low-paid workers, were unfit for active citizenship, as they were not fully "rational," justifying the exclusion of particular groups through denial of political power and/or civil rights as well as the granting of only partial citizenship. According to Arnold, people who are homeless lose "civil rights and enter a nondemocratic space" because they are perceived as being economic dependents or not making an economic contribution. The homeless who accept welfare or enter the shelter system are protected but still do not have rights. The homeless who do not assimilate to the system (e.g., by living on the street or in abandoned cars or vacant buildings) are criminalized and are therefore unprotected and lose rights. The notion of "citizenship," she argues, is based on economic criteria as well as social identity.[20]

The homeowner is one who has achieved self-preservation and is an autonomous and fully rational citizen. The homeowner has earned the right to certain privileges—including the very right to own property—by doing what is considered work (e.g., paid, full-time, and legal) and by having a family (e.g., two-parent, heterosexual, and economically independent).[21] The citizen is the one who is economically independent and makes a contribution to the market, while the political other is the one in debt and leeches off society. Clearly, the home has multiple symbolic connotations apart from literal shelter.

Homeless as Deviant and Dependent Nonpersons

Third boxcar, midnight train
Destination . . . Bangor, Maine.
Old worn-out suit and shoes,
I don't pay no union dues,
I smoke old stogies I have found
Short, but not too big around
I'm a man of means by no means
King of the road.[22]

The 1930s hobo is the stereotypical image of someone who is homeless: a man addicted to alcohol or drugs and too lazy to work. Before the nineteenth century, negative language, such as beggar, vagrant, pauper, rogue, and tramp, was used for anyone who was homeless. Later, the term *homelessness* was used more positively as a state of being without a home, yet the negative stigmas did not disappear.[23] Those who fall outside of the homeowner norm, especially people who are homeless, are routinely stigmatized and turned into the "other" by prevailing social myths that permeate our collective consciousness, including the ideas that: (1) people who are homeless are unreliable, incompetent, and mentally unstable; (2) people are homeless because of a personal fault or characteristic (e.g., laziness, addiction, lack of education, disability); (3) people are homeless because they choose to be homeless; and (4) people who are homeless need discipline and structure to put order in their lives.

Since so many organizations and so much public policy focuses on people who are chronically homeless (only a small number of the actual homeless), the image of a "homeless person" is the "diseased other." Geographer David Sibley maps how the poor in nineteenth-century cities were seen as sources of pollution and moral danger. They lived in slums with no sanitation and were subject to contagious diseases. In short, the poor represented excrement and disease that the rich left behind when they fled to the suburban heights. While sanitation has improved, homelessness today is still equated with pollution and deviance.[24]

Assigning the attributes of unreliability and incompetence to people who are homeless allows us to justify policies that criminalize rather than assist them, as the labels make them clearly undeserving of help. Brian J. Walsh and Steven Bouma-Prediger comment on Sibley's notion that "imperfect" people are put "elsewhere":

> The boundaries between the rich and poor are erected by the powerful in order to reduce the threat of their own defilement. Slums are *down*town as opposed to the suburbs which are *up*town. The topography of the poor is identified with filth, disease, excrement, and foul odors. And all of this legitimizes the ideological rhetoric of "cleanup campaigns."[25]

Attempts to clean up the city, whether in the nineteenth century, 1970s urban renewal, or today, can be seen as processes of purification aimed at excluding groups that are defined as polluting.[26]

Rather than focusing on structural causes of homelessness, such as shortage of affordable housing, changes in the economy, or prejudice, the dominant ideology encourages the idea that people are homeless because they have a personal fault. The number one fault is laziness; it is presumed that people who are homeless prefer to leech off the welfare system rather than work. Racism has always played a part in these images. For example, a prevalent image of blacks is unwillingness to work, of black men "dependent on the mothers of their children, the mothers themselves dependent on the largesse of government handouts."[27] Increasingly, sexism is playing a part, especially imputing disorganization, pathology, and laziness to single mothers who become homeless.[28] Many social scientists jump from evidence showing there is a prevalence of crime, long-term welfare, and homelessness in a particular area to the unsubstantiated claim that people who live in these areas have a "lack of will and commitment to get an education or a regular job."[29]

Another perceived fault is disability, often the result of addictions or mental illness. Vagrancy was seen as the primary disorder of homeless men at the turn of the century, but Howard Bahr, in his book on skid row, notes that later "vagrancy was superseded by alcoholism, and social control programs changed their focus from neutralizing

wanderlust to maintaining sobriety."[30] Doug Timmer and his colleagues note the class bias in associating homelessness with disability:

> When homeless people do have mental difficulties or problems with
> alcohol, these situations are identified as the cause of their home-
> lessness. But when well-housed middle-class or upper-middle-class
> people are mentally ill or alcoholic it is identified as an unfortunate
> situation requiring attention and treatment.[31]

Social-scientific research on homelessness since the 1940s has often
focused on mental illness, drug addiction, and alcoholism. The image
of the skid-row alcoholic still persists even though studies in the 1940s
found that alcoholics were a minority in the skid-row population.[32]

The history of our treatment of the homeless has been based on
an image of a troubled person. From the mid-1600s to the mid-1800s,
individuals received assistance only if they were seen as a public danger or nuisance (affluence could hide problems), and the response was
generally one of disposal, not assistance. People with mental problems
were treated the same as common criminals. By the mid-1800s to the
mid-1900s, we switched from criminalization to institutionalization,
diagnosing and treating the homeless with mental illnesses. Even after
World War II, "comprehensive plans for rehabilitation" were popular.[33]
Then, in the late-1900s, we deinstitutionalized our mental facilities and
defunded public provision of housing and housing assistance, often
leaving people to fend for themselves, despite the emphasis on "continuums of care" (comprehensive services from prevention to emergency
shelter to permanent housing)[34] in the 1990s.[35]

Another enduring perception about homelessness is that people
actually choose to be homeless, whether from a desire to be free of societal restriction, as the hobo image suggests, or due to personal inability
to measure up, as the alcoholic image suggests. The historical view that
homelessness is a choice was heavily supported by the Reagan administration in the 1980s. In his exit interview with David Brinkley, Reagan
professed that homeless people in Washington, D.C., sleep outdoors on
heating grates by choice.[36] Whether theorists romanticize (hobos) or
demonize (alcoholics) the homeless, they are agreeing that homelessness is to some extent a choice.[37]

People who work out of a belief that homelessness is a choice often assume that people who are homeless simply require more discipline and training in the virtues of hard work, temperance, and independence to influence different (e.g., "better") choices that will solve their situation of homelessness. The stated goal of many assistance agencies is to "empower" people to take greater control over their lives, supported by job training, self-esteem building, and twelve-step programs. Often, instilling discipline is seen as a path toward control. People are kicked out of shelters and programs for bad behavior because to do otherwise would be to enable them. People who are homeless often internalize the message that they simply need discipline and that if they can be sufficiently "disciplined," independence will follow.[38]

The 1987 McKinney-Vento Act has a not-so-subtle concern about the dependency of those who are homeless.[39] Congressman Clyde Holloway's comments in floor debate over the McKinney Act illustrate the worry about dependency:

> It is time that we stand together and say, "Listen, there are 10 million people out there who would love free housing." I am homeless if you want to look at it that way. It is time that we look at it and say, "What is the role of the Federal Government? What are we to do?" There is no end if we are going to keep offering candy bars. There is no end to the line that is going to line up and wait for candy.[40]

Concern over dependency led to an amendment to the act authorizing local communities to require "able-bodied homeless persons to work for their assistance" (a precursor to work requirements of welfare reform in 1996).[41] The assumption is that through work and enforced rules, people will be trained in what are often seen as "middle-class values" of responsibility, discipline, and individual initiative.

Constructing a "diseased other" serves to define normality and stability—being housed or homeless serve as moral boundaries between who is respectable/clean (e.g., the middle-class, heterosexual nuclear family) or diseased/dirty (e.g., the mentally unfit addict).[42] The "diseased other" view is often correlated with what is sometimes called the "old homeless," that is, the image of the single male vagabond. As I will illustrate in the next section, some literature is now identifying the so-called new homeless, especially women and children, some of whom are not considered responsible for their homelessness, but victims of misfortune.

Historian Cynthia Bogardin notes that since the 1970s most social policy regarding homelessness has been based on the half-truth that people who are homeless are in their predicament solely as a result of individual behavior (deviancy model). She writes,

> So little of homeless social policy had to do with housing and so much of it had to do with the presumed individual deficiencies of homeless people. So few of the resources America spent on homelessness went toward the provision of permanent and accessible housing, while so many went toward studying homeless people's characteristics, "rehabilitating" homeless people from their deficits, or warehousing them in shelters that are both costly and temporary.[43]

The view of the homeless as "diseased other" can permeate both harsh and benevolent responses to homelessness. Obviously, policies aimed at ridding the streets of the homeless are of this view, but even policies that are aimed at helping people who are homeless are often premised on a stereotypical negative image. For example, sociologist Ken Kyle shows that although the McKinney-Vento Act talks about the "homeless as greatly deserving to completely undeserving," it overwhelmingly portrays those who are homeless as irresponsible and incapable.[44] Even organizations that call for compassion can have such an image, as an Atlanta Union Mission Web site illustrates with the message "Touch the untouchables."[45]

Alternative Images of the Homeless

Homeless as Victims of Misfortune

> Yeah, I ran. I ran to get away from that house and the people in it. I wanted to be on my own without all the hassles. . . . Yeah, right so I ended upon the street. No job because I was too young; no place to

stay because I didn't have any money. So when this dude approached me I went with him. . . . You know the rest of the story.[46]

If the old homeless was the male alcoholic vagabond, the image of the new homeless is families, battered women, abused youth, and people who are mentally ill, categories of people who are perceived as victims of misfortune and deserving of assistance.[47] This representation of people who are homeless simply sees them as down on their luck, not deviant. As I argue in this book, attention to structural causes of homelessness is crucially important, whether it be rising unemployment, a declining safety net, the lack of affordable housing, abuse in families, closing of mental institutions, or the feminization of poverty. The problem with the "down-on-their-luck" representation is not its structural focus but its emphasis on the "homeless as victim" that leads to a more intense focus on "*individual* vulnerabilities rather than on the *institutional* roots of homelessness."[48]

One example of focusing on individual vulnerabilities is the body of literature that shows that people who are homeless have a history of traumatic victimization. In a 1988 study comparing homeless and housed mothers in Boston, 41 percent of the mothers who were homeless and only 5 percent of those housed reported physical abuse in childhood; and 41 percent versus 20 percent reported having been battered in at least one adult relationship.[49] One could make the case, however, that poverty, and not simply housing, accounts for the high figures. A 1991 study of fifty mothers who were homeless and fifty mothers who were housed and receiving Aid to Families with Dependent Children (AFDC) found that 89 percent had experienced some form of physical or sexual abuse in their families, with no significant difference between the two groups.[50] Either way, the focus is on the vulnerability and, presumably, the characteristics of the women, not the structural issues of poverty, abuse, and affordable housing.

An assumption in the down-on-their-luck representation of people who are homeless is that they are struggling to achieve what society defines as success, and therefore they have a desire to be a part of "normal" society and to achieve the American Dream. Elliot Liebow, in his book *Tell Them Who I Am: The Lives of Homeless Women,* describes the homeless from this lens:

> At the first sight, one wonders why more homeless people do not kill themselves. How do they manage to slog through day after day, with no end in sight? How in the world of unremitting grimness, do they manage to laugh, love, enjoy friends, even dance and play the fool? How in short do they stay fully human while body and soul are under continuous and grievous assault?[51]

As sociologist Amir B. Marvasti notes, "Sympathy is articulated by observing failed expectations of normality."[52] The dominant American point of view is that everyone should want a professional job and a suburban house, but it is not clear what the subjects' point of view is (even when ethnographers claim to be sharing the voices of the subjects, as Liebow faithfully tried to do).

A focus on victimization ought to lead to antipoverty strategies, but instead, charitable responses, particularly shelters and transitional housing, are often the only strategies pursued. There has been a body of literature that asks not what shelters can do *for* people who are homeless but what shelters do *to* people who are homeless. In particular, the critique is that shelters enclose, stigmatize, and construct the deviant "homeless," in comparison to "normal" (e.g., housed) subjects.[53] Marvasti conducted ethnographies at various homeless shelters and shows how *both* staff and clients produce a narrative representation of the "homeless client" to serve their varying purposes. He illustrates how staff divides the clients into *guests* and *nonguests* based on their openness or resistance to treatment. Marvasti writes, "The competition between guests and nonguests in the context of a rule-oriented status system stifles the possibility of fundamentally questioning the nature of social inequality, bifurcating a potentially unified group into segmented bodies who, ironically, live at the conscientious mercy of their 'rational' hosts."[54]

The staff members are concerned about "making good use of the charitable dollars" and thus make decisions, based on their perceptions, about who it is most useful to serve.[55] The clients are interested in receiving services and therefore project an image that sets them apart from the "deviant nonperson" stereotype of people who are homeless by focusing on their misfortune and "normalness." Marvasti notes that stories of medical disability, as well as unexpected financial and family misfortune, are institutionally acceptable ways to get aid.[56]

Homeless as Agents

> I've been homeless off and on since 1992. I went through three or four shelter programs before I figured out that they weren't the answer. The problem is that we are living in a country with a political system that supports poverty and homelessness. As a homeless person, I don't want charity. I don't want a shelter. I want political power. I want my human rights. (Dave, a person who is homeless)[57]

An alternative view to the dominant ideology does not ignore the victimization that the homeless face or the structural causes of homelessness, but focuses on the agency of the homeless, that is, on their ability to make rational choices in light of their circumstances.[58] Social geographer Susan Ruddick argues that the social sciences have succeeded in convincing the public that the homeless are victims of structural forces beyond their control, and thus have no agency. She sees the victim worldview as an improvement over the choice worldview but argues that the dichotomy between "homeless by choice" and "homeless as victims" risks furthering the assumption that, simply because people are subject to structural oppression, they are in turn incapable of political action. She claims that the public policy consequence of focusing too heavily on victimhood is that we conflate people with the "social pathologies that have in a sense 'produced them.'"[59] To illustrate, she critiques the shift in the women's shelter movement over the past twenty years, from a feminist focus on resisting systemic structures of sexism and patriarchy, to a rehabilitation focus of "treating the victim" to be "able to return to what is considered a 'normal and functioning (read homed) society.'"[60]

Ruddick's response is to examine the survival tactics used by people who are homeless: waiting for a bus to have a sheltered place to sleep, teamwork of one person working while the other guards possessions, women pretending insanity to avoid attack, and more.[61] Critics have been concerned that by focusing on the normalcy of people who are homeless we will give too much credit to the revolutionary potential of such resistance and begin to view homelessness as acceptable.[62] Ruddick does not downplay these concerns, but is fearful that in emphasizing homelessness as victimhood, we also risk viewing people who are homeless as incapable of political action. Numerous organizing efforts by people who are homeless show this latter perception to be invalid, yet the myth persists.[63]

Dominant Responses to Homelessness

Assimilate or Criminalize

> The homeless as radically free (as homeless by choice, their condition defined by resistance and a lack of subordination to social control) can either be invested with romantic longing or condemned as a dangerous class. Similarly, the homeless as unfree (as involuntarily homeless, their condition defined by necessity, constraint, and deprivation) can either be invested with sympathy, pathos, and fantasies of saving missions or excluded as "matter out of place." The most typical opposition is between a vision of the homeless as dangerously and profanely free (justifying criminalization) and a vision of the homeless as sacralized, helpless sufferers (justifying shelter). It is the opposition that . . . underlies the policy polarity between punishment and sanctuary.[64]

People who become homeless are subjected to assimilation or criminalization efforts, depending on how they respond to their homelessness, and depending on how the "helpers" perceive them. People who are perceived as victims of misfortune and are willing to be helped are deemed "deserving" and offered aid that aims to form them into responsible citizens who can be successful in our society. People who are perceived as making bad choices and causing their homelessness and/or are unwilling to cooperate with aid agencies are deemed "undeserving" and subjected to laws that criminalize them.

This ideology goes back as early as the Puritans, when the community cared for the deserving poor who were destitute due to no fault of their own, but bound the undeserving poor into service. Up until industrialization in the 1800s, charity (at least for the deserving) was generally understood as a religious duty. Communities were for the most part rural, and people cared for their neighbors in need. With industrialization, urban areas mushroomed, as did the number of people in need. The anonymity of urban life and the sheer number of people in poverty led to a fear of the poor, and stereotypes proliferated.

Two approaches to the poor and homeless developed.[65] One was a harsh moralistic position, which viewed all people who were homeless as lazy criminals who should be imprisoned. Providing assistance to such criminals would only encourage idleness. For example, in 1895 homelessness authority John McCook argued at the National Conference of Charities and Correction that the "tramp problem" should be solved through prison sentences and that hobo camps should be repressed so children would not be attracted to a life of vagabondage.[66] The only facilities for people who were homeless were in police stations.[67]

A more benevolent approach surfaced at the turn of the twentieth century, as unregulated capitalism produced more homelessness. Many religious organizations, such as the Gospel Rescue Mission and the Salvation Army, worked at reforming those who were homeless, often requiring work for room and board. The religious reformers saw the tramp as a "problem to be solved rather than a demon to be exorcized,"[68] and thus their mission was to inculcate a work ethic and virtuous character in conjunction with right Christian teaching. In the 1880s and until the 1930s, vagrants were made to "chop wood or break stone for a bed."[69]

Both the punishing and the reforming approaches assumed that those who were homeless had some sort of fault or deviancy that made them homeless, and both viewed those who were homeless as the "diseased and dirty other," as a quote from nineteenth-century literature attests: "There is a large class who must be regarded as outcasts, for whom the policy of sanitary regulation, of inspection, even of harrying, seems to be the only resource, and who must be regarded, in the mass, as hopeless subjects of reform."[70] Not until the Great Depression of the 1930s did public discussion of structural causes appear, from which the first federal program, the Federal Transient Service, was created to assist people who were homeless and unemployed.

Today, the criminalization and assimilation approaches remain prevalent. Beginning in the 1990s, cities have employed a number of punitive tactics to clean the streets of the homeless who are considered undeserving, namely those who struggle with addictions or mental illness and those with criminal records. For example, in 1994, New York City mayor Rudy Giuliani enacted "quality-of-life" ordinances whereby police could arrest people for sleeping or sitting on sidewalks. In 2005, Lawrence, Kansas, Atlanta, Georgia, and other cities passed antipanhandling laws.[71] As we have moved to a postindustrial order, political theorist Leonard Feldman notes a shift from older vagrancy laws that coerced the "idle" into the world of work to contemporary antihomeless laws that seek to exclude people who are marginal, since we now have less need for workers and are instead more interested in hiding abject poverty.[72] The homeless, according to Feldman, "deviate from all the social norms associated with status-seeking society," and are an eyesore on "middle-class consumptive spaces that are internally homogenous." As Eric Brosch puts it:

> A decade ago, when America was engaged in a genuine debate over the plight of the homeless, media images of tattered figures begging for change and sleeping on heating grates were omnipresent. Apparently debate is over; today the public wants the homeless out of sight and out of mind, and legislators have responded to our waning sympathy in kind.[73]

Thus, the antihomeless laws serve to purify public and private space from the "diseased other," thereby alleviating middle-class discomfort. Advocates of antihomeless legislation view such laws as "tough love," while others see them as political exclusion.[74] Advocates for the homeless argue that such criminalization has led to an increasing number of attacks on people who are homeless, primarily by young adult males.[75]

Simultaneously, homelessness has become a "social welfare growth industry"; that is, those who are homeless have become a new category of welfare client who must go through complex treatment protocols before gaining access to the scant transitional housing available.[76] Those who seek help and are willing to be "reformed" will be deemed worthy yet subjected to all sorts of rules and regulations on their lives. Social workers and staff at shelters often see the poor only at their most vulnerable, and as a consequence their stereotypes can be reinforced rather than challenged. Furthermore, such professionals have a vested interest in keeping their careers, thus they are more likely to propose reformist rather than radical agendas for transformation.[77]

The belief that people who are homeless need an array of services to address their personal problems has become deeply ingrained in the minds of many service providers. Some have opposed the new "Housing First" emphasis, which seeks to house people first and then offer services, because they feel it does not offer enough assistance from trained professionals for those who have problems such as addiction, mental illness, or extreme physical disabilities. In part, these service providers want to retain control over their "clients."[78] With HUD's "continuum of care" emphasis, public policy has focused also on reforming individuals over building affordable housing.[79] As Vincent Lyon-Callo remarks, "Individualized deviancy is at the root of contemporary responses to homelessness."[80]

Nicholas Retsinas, director of the Harvard Joint Center for Housing Studies, sums up our current focus in recent political campaigns, saying, "Two housing issues made it onto the polls: one was the need for more home ownership, and the other was 'Let's get criminals out of public housing.'"[81] That is, we support homeownership for the worthy middle class and policing for the unworthy poor. Our fear of dependency and our emphasis on individual responsibility means that anyone who is not economically independent will need to show worthiness to receive aid. After the Depression in the 1930s, we were aware of structural reasons for homelessness and set up some safety net entitlements to cover the vicissitudes of capitalism, but today we are more likely to blame the poor for their homelessness and support policies that increase homeownership over those that provide affordable rental housing.

Private or Public

> The affirmation of government, as the instrument through which the
> people of the nation carry out common aims and goals to see that
> the health, education, and welfare of all citizens are provided for, has
> been under assault in recent years. The individual interests of citi-
> zens and of corporations are set over against the government, which
> is described as somehow stealing from its citizens when it taxes them
> to resource services for the common good.[82]

Various views on homelessness correspond to our culture's changing
attitude toward individual and government responsibility. We can trace
a conservative stance from English vagrancy laws to the modern get-
tough ordinances against people who are homeless. This view holds
that individuals are responsible for their own well-being, and the state
is simply responsible for "negative" freedoms, that is, protection from
harm and protection of private property. A reforming stance holds
the government responsible for some aid to the poor, but as the alms-
houses of the 1800s illustrated, the aid was minimal and recipients were
expected to show themselves as deserving of aid through work, with the
end goal being rehabilitation from their idle and incorrigible ways. Most
aid was handled at the local level through the church and/or municipal
authorities, with a minimal government role.

By contrast, a liberal stance values a central and active role of government in poverty alleviation and aid. The earliest example of such a
stance was the U.S. pension program for Civil War veterans in 1862,
but it was not until the mid-1930s that comprehensive welfare policies
were put into place. A liberal stance holds that people are victims of
circumstances beyond their control, and thus the state has a responsibility to provide a safety net. Liberal policies were followed for fifty
years until the Reagan era, after which we moved away from a public
response to the problems of poverty and toward placing the burden for
socioeconomic success on individuals, with private organizations being
the safety net of last recourse.[83]

As evidence of our move away from public governmental response,
volunteerism is in vogue with both conservatives and liberals. Each

has a different rationale for promoting volunteerism, however. Ronald Reagan summed up the rhetoric of the conservative view: "We've let Government take away many things we once considered were really ours to do voluntarily out of the goodness of our hearts and a sense of community pride and neighborliness."[84] Underlying this rhetoric is a promotion of the private sector over expansion of the state (at least for poverty alleviation and safety nets for the poor) and a belief that voluntary action maintains traditional American values of free enterprise, hard work, economic growth, and discipline.[85] Implied is the notion that state provision of welfare will take away private initiative and be overly intrusive in people's lives.

Liberals see volunteerism as promoting grassroots participation and decentralization of power, as well as offering alternatives to marginalized groups, who are often oppressed by large-scale and professional service providers. Liberals envision numerous local decentralized voluntary alternative initiatives eventually transforming our capitalist society. Despite differing rhetoric, both conservatives and many liberals today concur that encouragement of private response over governmental involvement is good.

Welfare capitalism (capitalism with public-welfare supports such as Social Security, unemployment insurance, and Medicaid/Medicare) was originally supported by political and business leaders as a private, voluntary alternative to socialism. With the onset of the Depression, the voluntary sector could not adequately respond to need, and the business community was wary of growing public interest in a more socialist economy. Growth of the welfare state peaked in the mid-1970s, and for a number of reasons social-welfare expenditures as a percent of GDP have dropped significantly since then.

Taking the place of the welfare state is what political theorist Jennifer Wolch calls the "shadow state," that is, provision of welfare services by a private sector that the state regulates and subsidizes. While tax money still supports some welfare provision (although greatly reduced), the services themselves are not formally part of the state. Wolch points out the paradox that, despite the retreat of state intervention, we actually have an increasing penetration of state control via voluntary groups.[86] For example, voluntary groups that accept public money often find they lose their autonomously defined agenda, have less leeway to be critical of governmental policy, and lose flexibility and innovation in trying to achieve the values of efficiency and accountability. A more progressive perspective argues that the emphasis on voluntarism and empowering the poor by decreasing their "dependence," promoted by both Democrats and Republicans, hides the redistribution of wealth to the rich.[87]

Justification of Excessive Wealth and Inequality

> *Interviewer*: When you hear the phrase *the American Dream*, what do you think of?
>
> *Suzanne*: My initial reaction is, just know that we live in a country that's democratic and that anybody—given hard work—regardless of their economic background, has an opportunity. It's not dictated for them. And they can make it if they just have the right values and they have the drive, that they can do it.[88]

A key part of my argument is that we need to set the problem of homelessness within the framework of poverty, excessive wealth, and inequality. In other words, we need to challenge the inequality of power and wealth in our society if we are to have any chance of preventing homelessness and creating a sufficient amount of decent affordable housing. While we need to be aware of the ways in which we have created ideologies about the homeless and homeowners, we also need to understand the ideologies that justify the accumulation of extreme wealth by some while so many people struggle to get by. We might be tempted to call these "ideologies of the wealthy," but in truth people in all class levels uncritically adopt these ideologies, even if these ideologies work against their own class interest.

One of the more entrenched ideologies used to justify inequality is the belief in the American Dream of meritocracy, that is, that individuals achieve particular class positions solely on the basis of hard work or lack thereof, and that in America all who work hard can achieve the dream of financial success. Sociologist Heather Beth Johnson interviewed numerous families at different income levels on the subject of wealth inequality, but found that repeatedly the topic of meritocracy came to the forefront. She writes,

> They often initiated the subject [meritocracy] themselves and brought it up repeatedly. It seemed as though they knew at some level that by talking so openly about structured wealth inequality, they were somehow compromising the culturally sacred tenets of the American Dream that they believed in so strongly, and felt compelled to defend their beliefs.[89]

Both well-off and disadvantaged families in these interviews openly acknowledged a structure of wealth inequality and differing advantages and privileges yet nevertheless insisted that hard work and personal choices were the cause of social stratification in American society.

All the families used the American Dream to explain their current circumstances, the disadvantaged families claiming that they should have worked harder and made better choices, the advantaged families commending themselves for their hard work and initiative. The American Dream gave families hope, especially for their children, that although not everyone will make it in America, they will at least get an equal opportunity and a fair chance to succeed.[90] While most people realize that we do not all start life with the same advantages (e.g., good schools, neighborhoods, health care, families, and more money), and many understand that discrimination based on race, gender, and other group characteristics still exists, a majority of people still continues to believe that we are a society of equal opportunity and that everyone has a chance to make it if they work hard enough.

We disregard societal obstacles or advantages to success and instead view people as autonomous individuals independent of their social location. Johnson writes, "As a creed the American Dream represents a basic belief in the power and capacity of the individual."[91] In other words, if people have positions of power and own substantial wealth, then we assume they must be people of superior intellect, diligence, and character who used their talents wisely. No attention is paid to the structural inequities that gave certain groups a head start. In turn, we assume that people who are impoverished and marginalized must not have the innate capacities to take advantage of opportunities offered. No attention is paid to the structural inequities that kept certain groups from cultivating capacities for success. Instead, they are accused of lacking the skills, intellect, or middle-class mind-set that they never had the opportunity to acquire.

The better-off believe they have gained their social position through hard work and diligence alone because they are usually unaware of their unearned privileges. They are often unable to step out of their own social location and see that others do not have the same privileges, whether the privilege is living in a safe neighborhood, being treated with respect in a store, or fitting in with America's dominant culture. Social theorist Peggy McIntosh speaks of these privileges as "an invisible package of unearned assets that I can count on cashing in each day, but about which I was 'meant' to remain oblivious."[92] If the better-off are ignorant of their "backpack of assets," then they are more apt to believe there is a level playing field for all. They will often point to the handful of people who made it without unearned privileges, like Oprah Winfrey, to prove that equal opportunity exists.[93]

Another ideology that justifies the existence of extreme wealth in the hands of a few is the argument that inequality provides incentive for productivity and success. The opportunity to achieve greater material wealth provides incentive for competition and growth within an economy. With competition, people will be motivated to work harder and more innovatively to achieve success, in turn benefiting others through increased jobs and productivity. In addition, capital should be put in the hands of capitalist leaders and innovators, as they will wisely use science and technology to improve our lives and create better jobs for the general population. No mention is made of the 80 percent of the population who have seen their wages and benefits go down, nor is an argument made that this side of inequality is an incentive for success.

Still another way that inequality and excessive wealth are justified is by glorifying wealth and promoting the American Dream as desirable and good. Television programs like *Lifestyles of the Rich and Famous* and tabloid magazines chronicling Paris Hilton's every move are illustrative of the value we place on wealth. We do not generally blink an eye when we hear that CEOs make over four hundred times what an average factory worker makes. Only with the recent recession and government bailouts have we been upset that executives are paid handsomely when their companies are receiving tax money to avoid bankruptcy. We assume that such salary inequalities are the price for ingenuity and progress. Most people do not know that European and Japanese CEOs make considerably less than American executives. Most Americans do not critique excessive wealth but instead envision how they would live if only they won the lottery!

Most Americans also have no sense of the massive amount of wealth the rich actually have, nor are they aware of the means by which they achieved such wealth. We tend to focus on multidigit salaries of high-profile people such as Michael Jordan rather than on the accumulation of wealth. In 2007, the top 10 percent of Americans brought in almost half of all reported income, most of it money made from investments (not salaries), as they own more than 80 to 90 percent of all stocks, bonds, trust funds, and business equity.[94] The top 1 percent of the American population owns more than the bottom 90 percent combined![95] About one-third of the wealthy inherit their wealth, while another third benefit from inheritance, yet we believe the average Jane and Joe can make it into that elite circle with hard work.[96]

Conclusion

Understanding America's dominant ideologies on homelessness and housing is necessary for analyzing historical and current responses to homelessness. Many times we overtly label people using dualistic categories (e.g., good/bad, housed/homeless, clean/dirty), but often we unwittingly label the homeless as the dirty other simply by emphasizing an idealized image of respectable housed citizens. We also manage to subdivide further the homeless by labeling them deserving or undeserving. While these categorizations might seem philosophically abstract, they play a significant role in shaping how our society responds to homelessness and housing. As Christians, we must critically assess whether these ideologies are in line with our understandings of the gospel values of hospitality, love, and justice. In the following chapters on Christian responses to homelessness and housing, readers can begin the process of identifying when dominant ideologies are at play, whether they are helpful or hurtful, and how we might be more supportive of liberation.

While it is important to be aware of the dominant ideologies about the homeless and the housed, focusing only on these ideologies can distract us from the deeper issue of inequality and the extreme accumulation of wealth. Ideologies justifying inequality and ideologies about who is housed support an American Dream of meritocracy that assumes the social position people inhabit is mainly a result of individual decisions and character, not environmental factors. We have unfailing faith in the ideas of a level playing field and equal opportunity for success in American society. Thus, social and class position is an indicator of whether individuals worked hard enough or were intelligent enough to take advantage of the opportunities. In addition, the lure of making it big, fueled by our media and culture, is what offers incentive for the innovation, the drive, and the competitive spirit that promotes increased growth and productivity. Our emphasis on private volunteerism and decreasing the dependence of the poor are connected to our emphasis on individualism rather than a public communal emphasis.

Discussion Questions

1. Are there specifically American stories and values that influence how you view people who are either housed or homeless? How do these stories and values get reinforced theologically by Christian congregations?

2. Do you have examples of how a normative image of homeowners as responsible autonomous citizens has played out in our culture? Are there positive and negative implications of such an image?

3. How has the image of the homeless as deviant and dependent non-persons played out in our culture, and what are the implications of

this image? What are the different implications of the homeless as victims of misfortune or the homeless as agents?

4. Were you aware of our ideologies about public versus private response and our ideologies justifying excessive wealth and inequality? What are the implications of these ideologies for how we address homelessness and housing?

5. Are there stories and values within the Christian tradition and told within faith communities that offer alternative visions to some of the American ideologies that stigmatize and idealize particular groups of people in our society and that support inequality? How might we have an American Dream of hospitality, love, and justice?

-4-

Rescue and Recovery Response

Many traditional and government-funded approaches fail not for lack of money but for a deficit of vision: They do not treat the whole person. They neglect the familial and moral aspects of a person's life. They refuse to challenge the homeless person's fundamental way of thinking. . . . Most significantly, these programs ignore the central dimension of the problem—the spiritual.

—Rev. Stephen E. Burger, Executive Director, International Union of Gospel Missions, 1996[1]

I scoop the meat and gravy onto the disheveled man's cafeteria tray at the soup kitchen of a rescue mission. He then takes several rolls, three cartons of milk, and sits down at a table with five other men who are telling stories and joking. I scan the room and note that three-fourths of the diners are black men. I see only three women, two black and one white. At one table, a group of men are speaking Spanish. Later, I sit down with two homeless people, and although they courteously nod to me, they concentrate on eating and do not say much. After lunch I am introduced to one of the homeless women. She says to me,

I'm an alcoholic and am not working. I come here each day for meals. I need things to do to fill my time. People stole the money from us—in this country the wealth needs to be spread around. People in poverty are so beat down that they end up on drugs and alcohol. We don't want to help ourselves because we don't feel that we deserve it. We actually end up hurting ourselves.[2]

As I leave, I walk past the only picture on the wall, a portrait of the often-seen blue-eyed white Jesus. From there, I go to the family shelter where volunteers are watching kids in a colorful play area with monkeys swinging from trees on the jungle-painted walls. Some of the staff is doing a symbolic foot washing of the single mothers and giving them pedicures. Next door, the drop-in center is opening up after lunch, and a few homeless men come in and sit down for an afternoon of television. There is always something going on at AGRM (Association of Gospel Rescue Missions) missions.

Many Christians volunteer with religious organizations that provide charity to people who are homeless, and many churches, either alone or in coalition with other churches, provide soup kitchens, temporary shelter, and/or food banks. Although there were no other volunteers the day I was at the soup kitchen, homeless people in Christian-affiliated shelters are accustomed to seeing a wide array of church folk cycling in and out of various volunteer positions. To highlight a charity approach to homelessness, I will focus on one organization as a case study, the AGRM. I picked AGRM because it is a national religious organization with over three hundred affiliates that offer direct charity such as emergency shelter and soup kitchens. Many of the missions also have addiction programs, youth outreach, thrift stores, prison ministry, and transitional housing. Most church members volunteer through various programs that provide basic needs and offer visitation with people in prison.

My aim in picking a case study to examine is less to offer analysis of the particular institution than to highlight themes in the philosophy of the institution that might be similar for other institutions that focus on direct need. Despite the particularity of the AGRM's evangelical-to-fundamentalist theological perspective,[3] analysis of its ideas about charity and Christian responsibility offers insight into a wider array of Christian communities that respond to homelessness based on a charity model.

Association of Gospel Rescue Missions, formerly known as International Union of Gospel Missions, was formally established in 1913 but traces its roots back to 1872, when the McAuley Water Street Mission was opened in New York City. Former convict, river thief, and alcoholic Jerry McAuley stated of his rescue mission that "here, amid healthful and beautiful surroundings, many a drunkard has found Christ and redemption, and is now a happy Christian."[4] Thus, the founding purpose of this rescue mission was to save men who are homeless and alcoholic through spiritual renewal in Christ. For the most part, this has remained the focus, although recently there has been a small but growing offshoot of rescue missions that are emphasizing recovery more than rescue, and the rescue efforts have been extended to women as well (albeit slowly). As those missions that emphasize recovery put it, "two hots and a cot" is insufficient;[5] hard-core addicts need twelve-step recovery programs in addition to shelter.[6]

Rooted in an evangelical-to-fundamentalist theology,[7] the AGRM functions much like the Southern Baptist churches (where many of its members come from) in that each of its affiliate rescue missions operates quite independently from the national association, allowing for theological diversity. Beyond a common evangelical perspective, I encountered a diverse range of theological perspectives among staff. Some were more fundamentalist, with an authoritarian understanding of God, a literal understanding of Scripture, an emphasis on sin and depravity, and a message of obedience to God's authority. Others placed more emphasis on a compassionate God, a thematic understanding of Scripture, and a view of humans as God's children who might have put earthly desires before God but who can be transformed through the love of Jesus.

In this chapter, I will describe some of the themes that emerge from the literature and Web sites of a range of affiliate missions, the interviews I conducted with both staff and guests at five different rescue missions located across the country, and observations of institutional practices.[8] In particular, I will focus on AGRM's emphases on individual behavior as the cause of homelessness, and spiritual transformation and discipline as two of the solutions. I also will explain its perspective on race and gender analysis of poverty and homelessness. While there was theological diversity among staff at various AGRMs, most of them consistently emphasized the major themes that I have highlighted. I will try to convey the differences in perspective within each theme, however. My aim is to describe the themes that emerged and save analysis until later.

Before describing the themes, I would like to note that all of the staff and guests at the AGRM affiliates that I made contact with were extremely gracious and willing to share their perspectives and their stories.[9] Furthermore, all of the staff that I interviewed sincerely cared about the people they were serving, and all felt called by God to this ministry. Several of the staff I interviewed had themselves previously been homeless at some point in their lives. In addition to interviewing staff members, I interviewed guests in the different programs the various affiliates offered: (1) men and women in a homeless drop-in center; (2) men and women in addiction-recovery programs; (3) women in a two-year family shelter; and (4) women in transitional family housing. Many of the guests indicated that they had experienced hospitality and love during their stay at a rescue mission.

Individual Behavior as Cause of Homelessness

All of the rescue missions I visited had addiction-recovery programs, and all but one of the missions had an emergency shelter. While not all the men and women in the addiction programs have a history of homelessness, staff at the missions is in daily contact with people who are both episodically and chronically homeless and with people who have serious addictions. Thus, the people they serve tend to have a lot of personal problems. As one executive director said to me, "The people we serve are on the bottom rung of society. They have serious problems. They spit in your face; they don't want your help; they are a pain."[10] While staff members at mission affiliates see people who are transitionally homeless, their more sustained contact is with people who are chronically homeless and need more help.

This close contact with chronic homelessness influences one's outlook on homelessness and its causes. Despite numerous stories of poverty, oppression, and abuse, the perspective of both staff and guests at the rescue missions is that individual behavior is overwhelmingly, if not exclusively, the cause of homelessness. More guests than staff were likely to name structural causes of homelessness, but when asked a follow-up question on solutions to homelessness, they usually gave responses that addressed individual behavior, not structures or policies. For example, several guests identified low-paying jobs and lack of affordable housing as key causes of homelessness, but their main solutions involved addressing dysfunctional behavior so people could get and keep a job and providing more shelters to help people in need.[11]

In the interviews I conducted and in mission literature, addiction to drugs and/or alcohol is cited as the main cause of homelessness. One rescue-mission brochure cites: "A national study says 65%–85% of homeless adults have a substance abuse problem."[12] Their 2007 mission statement was "Meeting the needs; mind, body and soul; of those battling against addiction and homelessness, to break the cycle of *destructive behavior* [italics mine] that is passed from generation to generation."[13] This statement equates addiction with homelessness and identifies the problem as individual destructive behavior. The brochure of this affiliate states:

> They've lost their financial security, their homes, and in some cases, their family. Their lives are wracked by pain, the kind you can't simply heal with bandages and medicine. They're addicts. Broken people that have lost their way. They make up the overwhelming percentage of what society generally refers to as the "homeless."[14]

Retired executive director Stephen Burger (who served from 1989 to 2007) claims that 80 to 90 percent of people who enter most rescue missions show symptoms of substance abuse.[15] These statistics *might* be accurate for people coming to rescue missions (although the increase in families with children has probably lowered this number since cited in 1996), but many staff members claim these percentages for all people who are homeless.

Most rescue mission staff does not believe lack of affordable housing is the major problem. One executive director said, "The temptation is to be practical in social services—feed and clothe people. If they only have a house, everything will be fine. But we need to ask, 'Why don't

they have a house?' Housing is not the primary problem."[16] Stephen
Burger critiques government programs for assuming that homelessness
is "simply the absence of four walls and a roof," and not the result of
deeper issues like the breakdown of family and moral depravity. Burger
and other rescue mission staff contend that, without personal transformation, approaches to solving homelessness will fail.

One rescue-mission staff member advocated changing the name
of the institution to Association of Rescue and Recovery Missions.
He argued that focusing on "recovery" rather than "rescue"—that is,
emphasizing addiction programs over emergency shelters and soup
kitchens—is a more structural approach than simple charity. He claimed
that emergency shelters are simply enabling the homeless, as they do
not encourage behavior change.[17] A director of development of another
affiliate felt that her mission addresses the root causes of homelessness
by counseling each person one on one to find the individual reason for
their homelessness.[18] One of her staff said, "When I work with churches
there is a lot of enabling going on. Churches continually help with food,
but they need to send people to professionals who are trained to deal
with the deeper issues, and not just put a band-aid on the problems."[19]

While all staff felt their call was to help empower people to break
addictions and make the right choices, there were differing perspectives on why people were on a "path of self-destruction"[20] and without a
home. At one extreme was a view that all people are homeless because
they are living in sin and are wicked. One associate executive director
said,

> Most people are homeless because they are inherently lazy and
> wicked. Very seldom does a person become homeless because he
> lost a paycheck. . . . In a sense it is a choice. They continue to live a
> wicked life, not being accountable to anyone and they keep milking
> the system.[21]

A more compassionate view saw addictions as symptoms of deeper
issues such as abuse, poverty, or oppression. This latter view was more
prevalent when women and addiction were alluded to. One affiliate
brochure in explaining its program for women said,

Specially certified staff work with these wounded souls on a number of gender-specific issues, including mental, physical, emotional and sexual abuse. Counselors help women address issues related to shame, isolation, co-dependency and lack of boundaries.[22]

The emphasis of addiction programs, whether faith-based or secular, is on individual agency. The focus is to help people make healthy choices. Thus, even if staff had a more structural view of addiction, the aim of their programs is to transform individual behavior, not structures and policy.

Most often, bad behavior is depicted as a free choice that people make from selfishness and from following "their own way and not God's way." One brochure talks about the change in the average age of the homeless male from fifty-five in 1928 to early twenties today and says that the homeless male today suffers from "many forms of addiction: drug, alcohol, anger, sex." Following this claim, it depicts a guest saying, "This program has shown me that I cannot do anything without God. I tried it my way, and it didn't work."[23] In an affiliate newsletter, one guest says, "I was constantly pursuing the wrong things in an attempt to fulfill my selfish desires. That led me to make some really bad choices."[24]

I could never tell if guests I interviewed came to the rescue mission with this perspective or if they had simply learned it from staff. After telling his story of being fed liquor in his bottle, providing for himself by age nine, and spending three years in a youth home, one guest said, "I was homeless because I had to have things my own way. I had pride."[25] Another guest spoke of leaving home at age fourteen to get away from an abusive father, living on the streets from age fourteen to eighteen, and getting addicted to crack cocaine, yet ended her story by saying, "I chose to be homeless. I didn't want responsibility."[26] This guest also talked about having to work two or three jobs to deal with the cost of living and rents of $900 per month and about not having time for her three young children. Yet she blamed herself and not the structures that made getting by so difficult: "I could not handle single parenthood emotionally or financially."[27]

Testimonies from graduates of the programs are regularly found on affiliate Web sites and in affiliate newsletters. The common feature in all of the testimonies is an emphasis on bad personal choices. In an affiliate newsletter, a white female graduate recounts, "As a child I had a good home. But as I got older, I felt shy and struggled to fit in because I was always aware that I was different. When I became a teenager I experimented with drugs to fit in. . . . I was lost and now I'm found."[28] On an affiliate video, a black male says, "I knew if I tried something I was going to like it. I always knew I had addictive behavior." Never mentioned in the numerous testimonies are life experiences connected to homelessness, like growing up in poverty, attending schools that are little more than holding tanks, dealing with racial oppression, or experiencing emotional, physical, or sexual abuse.

When these details are presented, there is usually a focus on the individual's or family's learned "culture of poverty" and little emphasis on the structural aspects of poverty and oppression. Many rescue mission affiliates have an emphasis on "breaking the cycle of homelessness and poverty" based on the assumption that children learn helplessness from parents who are homeless, making them more likely to become homeless adults.[29] In fact, staff at two different affiliates found helpful a book called *Bridges Out of Poverty*. This book helps professionals understand the "hidden rules" of poverty, middle class, and wealth. The goal is for professionals to help people in poverty to adopt middle-class virtues and behavior as a "bridge" out of poverty. Although the introduction to the book notes that poverty is increasing due to structural reasons, the authors nevertheless emphasize changing individual "patterns of behavior" that are a result of generational poverty.[30] One staff member who recommended the book said, "People in poverty speak a different language and have different values. If we can teach them how to speak and act like middle America, they are going to be able to stop the cycle of generational poverty."[31]

Spiritual Transformation

While there were different theological perspectives on the exclusivity of Christianity (Jesus Christ as the only route to salvation) among staff, all claimed spiritual transformation as the emphasis of rescue missions.

Two of the missions I visited even substituted "ministries" for "rescue" in their names, as they felt evangelism was their primary purpose. Most rescue missions refuse government funding so that they can intentionally address the spiritual component of recovery, even mandating chapel attendance to stay in their emergency shelters. One affiliate I visited accepts government funding for its shelters but not for its addiction programs. Although they were interested in spiritual transformation as well, they claimed to be more interested in modeling Christ's behavior than preaching it and did not make chapel mandatory for shelter guests.

All affiliates believe addressing spirituality is a part of promoting wellness. Some affiliates claim being "born again" in Christ is necessary, while others place more emphasis on the love and acceptance that a relationship with Christ brings. An executive director with the latter perspective said,

> Relationship to Christ is so personal; you can't force it. It is internal, and has to be voluntary. We don't have them sit through a sermon to get a meal as that starts the whole relationship with Jesus on the wrong foot. Every point of contact for our guests should be of love. We do this through who we hire. The truck driver or chef needs to be just as interested in Jesus as the chaplain.[32]

What both perspectives on spirituality hold in common is an understanding of a personal relationship with Jesus as central to a deeper spirituality.

The perspective of the overwhelming majority of the staff that I interviewed is that the cause of homelessness is mainly spiritual, not economic.[33] While a few staff noted economics as a factor, their solutions to the problem of homelessness always focused on transformation of the individuals who are homeless, not transformation of economic policies or structures. For example, former executive director Stephen Burger acknowledges that the lack of affordable housing is an issue, yet writes, "After more than 35 years of trying to help homeless people with every imaginable problem, I cannot escape this fact: Men and women who walk away from their jobs, their families, and their homes do so because, fundamentally, they are turning away from God and His claim on their lives."[34] One executive director at a mission said that clients have all sorts of different problems but that they are all spiritual problems and that if they would just turn their lives over to Christ, Jesus can change them.[35]

Videos on affiliate Web sites are often shot like short *Extra* or *Entertainment Tonight* television clips depicting the miraculous healing when guests make the decision to accept Christ into their lives. One "True Rescue Mission Story" pictures "con artist superb" Jeremy Verret stepping off a bus in Raleigh and recounting his bad upbringing— parents divorced when he was nine years old, abused by his stepdad, and consistently shuffled around. The low point in his life was when he stole the last $400 his sister had to feed her three small children until her next welfare payment. Then Jeremy "finally allowed God to take over and his life changed." The end result: "Today Jeremy is living the American Dream. He is a manager of Five Guys, is very successful, has a family, and is very active in his church."[36]

Despite the miracle emphasis of testimonies in videos and newsletters, not all guests have such an instant life change. For many, relapse is part of the process of finally getting to wholeness. As one staffperson, formerly a guest, said to me, "I used to think that I'd have to be struck by lightning, but it was a process—in God's time things will change."[37] An associate executive director argued that failing is not final and offered his definition of success: "Failing forward without losing your enthusiasm."[38]

Some affiliates emphasize addiction as sin, while others see addiction as a disease. An executive director who believes in the former claimed people who are homeless are simply reaping the consequences of their actions.[39] For him, the root of homelessness is sin; thus, what the homeless need most is forgiveness of their sins. As one guest testified, "I was a rotten sinner in need of God's saving grace. The Lord pulled me up out of the miry clay and set my feet upon a solid rock."[40] Another staff member explained that, biblically, addiction is a sin. He went on to say that if addiction is simply a disease, then people have no responsibility for changing. They are simply born with it and have no choice in the matter.[41] He felt that confronting the sin with love gives people hope.

This same staff member said that his affiliate's teaching was "not to be sober, but to be clean." He said, "Being sober one can refrain from drugs and alcohol for a season but deep inside is still struggling because he is not clean from within [of the Holy Spirit]." For him, being "clean from within" is not about changing behavior but about changing a belief system. A new orientation in belief will change one's behavior. He aims to instill a biblical worldview that will "empower them [addicts] to resist temptation because it is not just about them, but about sinning against God."[42] As one guest testifies, "I wanted a new life. *God gave me that new life.* I wanted the cravings to go away. *God removed all my desire for drugs.*"[43] The affiliates that emphasize the addiction-as-sin model place more emphasis on a literal interpretation of Scripture, the depravity of human nature from birth,[44] and the importance of formally accepting Christ to wash away one's sins and be forgiven.

A handful of affiliates critiques the addiction-as-sin model as shame-based and prefers Alcoholics Anonymous's emphasis on addiction as a disease. Staff members at these affiliates think the homeless need acceptance and grace more than forgiveness. They claim that the homeless usually need to forgive themselves and feel that they are worthy of being loved by God before they are fully able to accept God's grace. A guest testimony uplifts the difference that a perspective of love and grace meant to her: "They taught me what love was about. And that God was a forgiving God. No matter how far down the scale I went God still loves me."[45] Another guest said to me, "I was very angry with God. I came here to fight God, now God is my friend. I've been taught that I'm worth his love, worth being a good person. I was never told as a kid that I was okay, pretty, smart."[46]

The staff in one addiction recovery program for women emphasizes the "spiritual" over the "religious." For them, this means being in relationship with God and one another over following legalistic rules of the church or God. They teach the women that spiritual wholeness, and in turn recovery, is about a personal relationship with God apart from religious icons, doctrine, and rules. To help women identify with God, the executive director has them put a pin on their bra to represent God (the God within whom they can talk to).[47] An executive director at a different affiliate said that reaching out with the grace and love of God and encouraging faith is critical for people who are homeless, as there is no physical or financial solution that will heal the hurt and sense of rejection they feel.[48]

One staff member noted, however, that 75 percent of AGRM staff nationwide is threatened by seeing addiction as a disease and not a choice because they think the model negates individual responsibility for sinful behavior.[49] Staff members who adopt the addiction-as-disease model hold that guests get the message of comfort while also being held accountable for their actions. This perspective also emphasizes the individual's ability to turn away from sinful ways and with God's help stop the addiction. Those who hold the addiction-as-disease model claim that it is in "God's power to deliver individuals from the compulsion to drink and abuse drugs," but recognize that in a therapeutic sense, former addicts will still be alcohol or chemical abusers.[50] Despite which model staff adopts, a concern about guests being "saved" prevails. As one executive director said to me, "The main reason we combine the most successful recovery program (12 Steps and the Bible) is that I have a fear that one day, one of our clients may find themselves sober and in hell."[51]

Many staff and guests said that relying on God gives strength to recover and gives purpose in life. Several guests claimed it was empowering to give up their worries to God and know that "He" will take their misfortunes and turn them to good. As one guest-turned-staff said, "Trust in God and He will provide. Sometimes I worry and then I remember that He always has my back."[52] She and her colleague said that people who have been homeless understand that God took care of them and know that they did not make it on their own. Several guests spoke of God using their past to give them purpose in the future. One woman who survived extreme domestic abuse said, "I decided if I survived I would speak for women who could not speak for themselves and spend days loving people I serve."[53] Another guest who survived seven drug-related gun shootings and called himself "Walking Dead" trusted that his experiences would help him in church leadership: "I have no regrets about what I have gone through—maybe I wouldn't have found God. All of my life is predestined. We always must be encouraged by stories and tell people to try Jesus."[54]

A key component of AGRM's spiritual emphasis is connecting guests in their addiction and housing programs to a church community. Most of the guests in the addiction programs have alienated people and have no family or community of support left. One guest said, "We don't want people to know us."[55] Rescue-mission addiction programs are usually only six months to a year, with family shelters and transitional housing lasting up to a year or two. As one staff member said, "We are expert at cleaning them up, but we need to hand them off to someone in the community."[56] Staff members believe that connecting formerly homeless people to churches is crucial to their long-term spiritual and physical well-being.

Although guests are welcome to go to any church they want, there are often a few churches that have employed people in recovery and therefore have a close connection to the local rescue mission. Some affiliates even have "covenant partners" who provide mentors and are more open than most churches to having formerly homeless members. As one guest told me about the church requirement, "I was wary at first because we're known as the 'people from the mission,' but the pastor said he had been where we are and then I felt better."[57]

Several staff criticized other programs, especially government-run programs, for not addressing spiritual transformation. One executive director said that we need practical solutions since housing costs money, but just focusing on the practical fails. Stephen Burger writes,

> For people dealing with alcoholism, drugs, guilt and frustration, no amount of training is going to help. At the Gospel Mission, we can talk about things government agencies can't address. We can tell people about forgiveness and moving on and right relationships with God, self, family and community.[58]

Two affiliates I visited connected attention to cleanliness to spiritual dignity. One director noted that another shelter in town did not paint their walls or fix things up and recounted a quote from a staff member of this shelter: "They don't care, why should we?" This director argued that beauty is important for spiritual transformation. "In our New Life Center there is a fountain in the waiting room. If homeless men are sitting there, they should be at peace."[59] For this director, creating a beautiful and clean environment shows a respect for the human dignity of guests. While spiritual transformation comes from within, how people are treated affects the possibility for such change.

In contrast to the AGRM's emphasis on spiritual sin or brokenness, the guests did not claim the causes of homelessness to be simply spiritual but frequently cited economic factors when discussing their own experience of homelessness. In fact, the common denominator in all of their stories was a childhood of poverty and, for many, abuse. One woman told me she felt homeless her whole life, as her family always moved from one place to another. When she was seventeen, she and her mom were evicted and ended up on the street. Before coming to the family shelter with her son, she slept pregnant on the floor with other family members.[60] Another woman grew up with an abusive and alcoholic father, her mother having died at a young age.[61]

Discipline to Avoid Dependency

The value of compassion was important at all the rescue missions I visited, but staff members understood it differently depending on the assumptions they held. Many staff members believed in a "culture of poverty" and felt people are homeless for lack of discipline and work ethic and for having learned the bad habit of dependency on charitable handouts. Although these staff members aimed to empower people in poverty, they assumed that the homeless are unlovable, nobodies, and friendless. As one male host says on a rescue-mission video, "We are committed to being here and reaching out to the people that nobody wants, to loving the unlovable, to making sure that people have the opportunity to turn their lives around."[62]

Some rescue missions had a heavy emphasis on discipline and work. One executive director at an affiliate boasted that the men are working all the time at his mission. He argued that it teaches them to become responsible, that life is not free, and that the mission does not simply give handouts.[63] He said that the guys do not always want to be held responsible but that the mission does not lack numbers coming in.[64]

In critiquing lax government shelters and promoting the strict regimen and tough love of rescue missions, Burger writes, "The homeless need an environment in which they are challenged to acknowledge and consistently renounce unhealthy behaviors; otherwise, they won't acquire the practical or emotional skills they need to succeed."[65]

In another article, Burger argues for a balance of love and law:

> On one hand, the Bible says if a man [sic] does not work he should not eat. Certainly if we always spare people from the consequences of their own behavior, they may never change. Like the prodigal son in the pigsty, people have to decide for themselves when they've had enough and are ready to change. But at the same time, we want to be benevolent and kind and demonstrate God's love through our compassion.[66]

One staff member related the tensions she felt in trying to uphold this balance between love and law:

> It has been a struggle for me as to whether it is a Christian act to ban someone from the shelter. This is God's house, a mission house. The clients are guests and guests follow the rules in someone's house. We need to hold them accountable. I struggle with when enough is enough. Before we ban anyone, every staff member meets with the person and prays with him or her, and then decides what is best for the general population.[67]

Not to enforce consequences, she felt, would simply enable destructive behavior.

Even guests testify to their lack of discipline before being "rescued." One guest writes, "As a Marine I was tough—but discipline was another story. . . . In the civilian world there is even less discipline."[68] Another guest says, "Having a schedule and routine is new for me. A lot of people are procrastinators and I'm the world's worst."[69] The executive director, who emphasized discipline and structure at his mission, remarked on the irony of trying to make people responsible while also making most of their decisions for them. He solved this apparent inconsistency by saying he wanted to have a class on decision-making skills for the guests.[70]

Other affiliates did not put as much emphasis on work but agreed that it was important to teach the homeless to follow rules. A former guest who now worked full-time in a mission warehouse said, "Many of the guys have never had a job. Their lifestyle caused everyone close to them to close the door. That [closing the door] is necessary because too many people enable. They [the guests] need to hit rock bottom."[71] Differently said, no one has held them accountable to rules, thus an atmosphere of discipline is what they need. One former guest-turned-staff said that many guests do not have boundaries or structure in their lives. She said that she used to stay up all night, sleep all day, and let a lot of people stay with her.[72] One director argued, "We don't just lead people by rules, but by good principles from the Word of God." He went on to say that "once they [guests] get to a more mature level, they can be less bound by rules. Until then, the rules help."[73] Guests in addiction programs, long-term shelter care, and transitional housing are required to work with case managers in setting goals and achieving them.

Race and Gender Neutrality

Race and gender analysis of homelessness and poverty, of leadership within AGRM, or of dynamics between staff and clients was notably absent in all of the affiliates I visited. I was told by the executive assistant to the national office that AGRM does not have racial and gender demographics of affiliate staff and boards of directors; therefore, my comments come from on-site and Web-site observations. The executive directors, unless it is a women's shelter, are for the most part male (and white).[74] While there is racial diversity on staff, it nowhere near parallels the racial makeup of guests.[75] Seventeen of nineteen faculty members of the online City Vision College, which was until recently AGRM's Rescue College, are white.[76] Yet when I asked staff about racial and gender inequities within mission affiliates, none of them identified racial or gender disparity in leadership.

The only gender disparity any of the staff identified was that most of the services were for men and not women (although this is slowly changing at some affiliates). None of the staff saw sexism or patriarchy as a problem in their affiliate, and most were not concerned about such problems in the national organization.[77] Yet, until 2010, one could find on the national AGRM Web site resources such as the pamphlet "Addressing Immorality," which blames poverty on illegitimacy and instructs women to reclaim their chastity and be sexually responsible by not giving away what "belongs" to their future spouse.[78]

The overwhelming response I got to questions about race was that they treat everyone the same; therefore, there is no discrimination. All of the staff equated racism with unequal treatment and did not articulate any awareness of cultural and/or institutional forms of racism. The staff in one woman's program claimed that most racial animosity is between light- and dark-skinned black women, not between staff and guests or between guests of different racial identities.[79] Another staff member said that when he started working at his affiliate, there were gang animosities based on racial identity, making it difficult for guys to share in groups. He basically "cleaned house," and some staff who did not agree with his stance ended up leaving.[80] In both of these responses, staff saw racial prejudice in the guests but not in their own behavior or institutional practices.

When I asked staff whether they thought their institution addressed race and gender inequities in society, most of them did not understand my question and claimed that they treated everyone equally and had no problem with racism or sexism within their own rescue mission. A few understood the question and said that in serving the poor they were addressing racial inequities in society, and by having family shelters they were addressing gender inequities in society. One staff member really did not understand what I was asking and went on to explain his belief that there were more African Americans in the program because they have no culture of shame. He said, "It is a glorification to talk about sin in certain cultures. . . . In black culture it is often cool to get in trouble." This staff person felt there were just as many people with addictions in Asian or Middle Eastern cultures, but because of a cultural emphasis on shame, depravity was kept private behind closed doors. So although he thought it was good to deal with addictions and sin early (shame can inhibit seeking help), he also thought that without shame, people do not mind falling back into their depraved ways.[81]

Conclusion

Churches of all different denominations and theological persuasions work with homeless shelters, soup kitchens, and food banks, and clearly not all Christians or church congregations will exhibit or relate to every theme that emerges from affiliates of AGRM. Nevertheless, these themes are common enough in direct-charity responses by church communities and individual Christians that it is helpful to highlight them for critical analysis. AGRM affiliates tend to locate the cause of homelessness in the individuals themselves. Therefore, the focus is on transforming individuals, both their spiritual perspective as well as their irresponsible behavior. AGRM staff aim to inculcate middle-class values, with an emphasis on discipline and work. Their goal is for guests to achieve a lifestyle of independence where they are able to take care of themselves. AGRM staff works to treat all guests equally, and as a consequence they claim that they do not participate in any form of race or gender discrimination.

Since AGRM affiliates are in contact with a large number of chronically homeless individuals and people with debilitating addictions, they are usually dealing with individuals who need to make changes in their lives. A greater spiritual connection and transformed behavior are often important pieces of recovery to wholeness. AGRM staff is exhibiting God's call to compassion by walking with people, many of whom would not make it on their own without assistance. In some areas, rescue missions offer the only programs for addiction recovery that are free of charge for homeless and low-income individuals. While AGRM's approach does not address structural factors causing poverty and homelessness, it admirably tries to empower individuals from within to live independently.

Discussion Questions

1. Has your faith community been involved in direct charity as an approach to homelessness? Share stories of your experiences with this approach.

2. What are the positive and negative implications of focusing on individual behavior as the main cause of homelessness? Do you have examples of this emphasis in the direct-service approaches you are familiar with?

3. What are the positive and negative implications of spiritual transformation as a component of addressing homelessness? Are there different ways that this emphasis can be promoted?

4. What are the positive and negative implications of an emphasis on discipline and independence? Are there ways to advocate responsibility without buying into our culture's oppressive ideologies?

5. How can faith communities offer charity as a response to homelessness without blaming the victims and focusing solely on transforming the homeless? How do we exhibit God's compassion and walk in solidarity with people in their recovery to wholeness?

Low-Income Homeownership Response

> I have always felt that a house is to a human family what soil is to a plant. You can pull a plant up out of the soil, pour all the water in the world on it, give it plenty of sunlight, and it will eventually die because it is not rooted. A plant needs to be rooted. A family is like that. If a family is not rooted, it will not flourish. It will not grow . . . will not blossom. But once a family is well-rooted, all kinds of wonderful things will begin to happen.
>
> —Millard Fuller, Founder, Habitat for Humanity[1]

My daughters and I stand under the rain-soaked canopy watching the dedication of the sixteenth Habitat house in a new housing development. After being handed a housewarming Bible, the Asian American single mother, with tears of joy, says how much this house will mean for her and her three children. While experiencing her excitement, I also twinge from the soreness in my back after shoveling rocks a few days earlier to backfill around the pipes of a Habitat house still under construction in another development of nine new homes. The twenty or so college students with whom I worked—all of them white—are spending their last day of their spring break "build" experience admiring the new Habitat houses with perfect lawns. In addition, one or two other families from this development come to see their neighbor's new home. Forty children of all races will play in the newly laid grass and ride their bikes down the smooth sidewalk. As the executive director of this affiliate said, "It is like a small United Nations—five languages spoken and very diverse. The kids have a wonderful time together."[2]

Many Christians realize that no matter how much charity they offer in response to homelessness, many people simply cannot afford a secure place to live. Generally, volunteers from churches do not have the time or the expertise to build affordable, safe homes, but they can and do in coalition with other churches and nonprofits. There are many forms this approach can take, from providing low-cost rental housing to helping people actually own homes. Some churches have formed their own community development corporations (CDCs) to invest and build affordable housing, while others opt to participate with already-existing organizations that construct low-income housing.

I have chosen to focus on Habitat for Humanity as a case study since numerous individual Christians and church communities have volunteered with them and because they are an international organization with over 1,700 affiliates in the United States.[3] I do not aim to do a full analysis of Habitat for Humanity, since others have undertaken that task.[4] Rather, my goal is to identify, and later analyze, some themes in Habitat's philosophy and practice that might be insightful for individuals and institutions that utilize this type of approach to homelessness and housing.

Millard and Linda Fuller founded Habitat for Humanity in 1976. Along with biblical scholar Clarence Jordan, the Fullers developed the idea of "partnership housing," where those in need of adequate shelter would work alongside those who have extra time and resources to build simple, decent homes. The program would be modeled after the "Economics of Jesus," that is, no profit and no interest would be charged for home loans from the revolving Fund for Humanity. Since its inception, Habitat for Humanity has built more than 200,000 homes in more than 3,000 communities worldwide.[5]

Habitat's stated goal is to "eliminate poverty housing from the face of the earth."[6] This goal addresses homelessness as well as substandard housing. The title of one of Fuller's books, *No More Shacks!*, illustrates the latter. Habitat does not really address homelessness on the front line, however. As one executive director of a Habitat affiliate put it, "We're the second level in addressing homelessness. There needs to be an entry level of shelters and transitional housing as well."[7] Habitat does not really serve the poorest of the poor either because Habitat home-owners have to be working and able to make payments on a home loan. Most affiliates pick families whose income is from 30 to 60 percent of the median income of their local area.[8] For example, in 2010, Habitat family income is generally somewhere between $24,000 and $49,000 in Seattle, Washington, and between $20,000 and $40,000 in Charlotte, North Carolina.[9] Habitat does make a world of difference, however, for many families who would not otherwise have been able to buy a home.

Just as AGRM has separate rescue missions, Habitat also has sepa-rate affiliates that are self-sustaining, each following the Habitat ethos and strategy but open to theological, and even religious, diversity. Although Habitat continues to describe itself as a Christian organi-zation, it is quite open to a coalition of differing theological and reli-gious perspectives in its staff, volunteers, and homeowners. Despite the diversity of affiliates, there are identifiable themes that emerge from Habitat literature and practice. The description of these themes comes from books written about the organization (several by Millard Fuller), the organization's national Web site, interviews I conducted with both staff and homeowners at five different Habitat affiliates located across the country, and the observations I made of the institution's practices.[10]

While there has been much written on Habitat's theology and prac-tice, I will focus on its rationale for emphasizing homeownership to address poverty, its image of the ideal family, the importance of sweat equity to its philosophy, its strategy of changing the consciousness of the rich, and its belief in building communities of commonality. Similar to the previous chapter, I aim to describe several themes that emerge and save analysis for the following chapter.[11]

I was inclined to appreciate Habitat's work, as I had heard about the organization for years from my grandfather, who in retirement was actively involved in building Habitat homes and served on the board of his local affiliate. On my grandfather's wall was a framed picture of himself with President Jimmy Carter next to a hammer Carter used at a Habitat build. Both Habitat staff and families, who took time from their busy schedules to share their understanding of Habitat's ministry and stories from their experiences, graciously received me. I felt a sense of camaraderie participating in builds and heartfelt joy watching a family move into their new home. I even learned how to seal and frame windows!

Homeownership as Transformative

An abiding theme in Habitat literature, reiterated by Habitat staff, is the transformation to both individuals and communities that homeownership can bring. Hence, Habitat's oft-cited motto: "Building houses, building community." Fuller devoted a whole book, *More Than Houses: How Habitat for Humanity Is Transforming Lives and Neighborhoods,* to extolling the benefits of homeownership with story after story of how families and neighborhoods have been transformed. The Habitat Web site also has "Homeowner Stories" that function much like AGRM's testimonies to show the success of the program in transforming individuals and, in Habitat's case, families. Fuller holds that "unbelievable changes occur when people have homes of their own."[12]

In his book, Fuller cites many benefits of homeownership. Not only will homeownership increase income, lead to a better quality of life, and give families a piece of the American Dream, it will also set them up for success; give them pride; break a cycle of welfare; and promote cleanliness, self-sufficiency, and a spirit of giving back.[13] On Habitat's Web site it says,

> Habitat for Humanity has shown that building homes does more than put a roof over someone's head. In clean, decent, stable housing:
>> Families can provide stability for their children.
>> A family's sense of dignity and pride grow.
>> Health, physical safety, and security improve.
>> Educational and job prospects increase.[14]

Executive directors I interviewed overwhelmingly emphasized homeownership as a means of wealth creation through equity. They also mentioned stability and a sense of control and independence that secure homeownership can engender.

Even greater emphasis is given to the ways homeownership increases the well-being of children. The current executive director, Jonathan Reckford, claims the children of homeowners do better in school, are safer, are less likely to become pregnant as teenagers, and have fewer behavior problems than children of renters.[15] The Habitat Web site quotes housing expert Lisa Harker: "Childhood is a precious time when our experiences shape the adults we become—but children who grow up in bad housing are robbed of their future chances."[16]

Consistently, I heard that homeownership gives children stability, while renting does not. One executive director said,

> When you bring stabilization to a family, it is not just for this genera-
> tion, but is impacting the next generation. Families are no longer in a
> cycle of renting housing all their lives. You see kids of families gradu-
> ate top of their class in high school and go on to college. One sponsor
> we have will only sponsor families with young kids because they want
> to see the difference it makes in the children's lives.[17]

This director said the mantra of the old days was building homes, but now the focus is more on families served. A study commissioned by Housing and Urban Development (HUD) and conducted by Applied Real Estate Analysis, Inc. (AREA), concluded that "all aspects of the Habitat program are structured to nurture families and break the poverty cycle—not just provide an affordable house."[18]

The story of Dorothy Howard illustrates the theme of stability and security of homeownership in contrast to the instability of generational poverty (and rental housing): "In 1988, two days before Christmas, she moved herself and her nine grandchildren out of a neighborhood that had become riddled with drug activity and into the stability not only of a Habitat house, but of homeownership as well." The Web site compares Howard's homeownership to the oak tree planted in her yard, noting that Howard learned a lot through homeownership, including the "intangibles such as community and permanence, security, stability and the awareness that family—her grandchildren, all adults now—can and do return home to the same place on Rawley Street in Houston."[19]

Stories of success from Habitat families clearly show measurable benefits to homeownership. At least some Habitat families have moved into the ranks of the middle class from home-equity savings. As one executive director said, "By owning a house, low-income people don't just jettison into another income bracket, but they can build equity, plus the other benefits of homeownership. Homeownership shouldn't just be for rich people."[20] A Vietnamese family paid off their twenty-four-year Habitat mortgage in nineteen years and was able to help three of their four children start their own businesses.[21] Another homeowner refinanced her Habitat home loan to pay for her daughters to go to college.[22]

There are also stories of improved health. For a New York family, a move from a "ramshackle apartment" with windows covered in black mold to a Habitat house solved their youngest child's life-threatening asthma.[23] A Florida mother knew that "her mobile home, with its poor air quality and lack of adequate air conditions, would not provide her son with the environment he needed to heal after the hospital stay." Her Habitat home not only helped her son heal but also lifted her spirits and gave her a "light at the end of the tunnel."[24] One Habitat affiliate received a thank-you note from a recent homeowner who said in her previous life she had been in and out of hospitals for respiratory illness, but since moving into her Habitat home she had not used her inhaler even once.[25]

The literature and staff also promote the idea that homeownership brings pride and even spiritual transformation. In Habitat's online publication *Habitat World*, a woman writes, "My children had a home they could take pride in. They were no longer embarrassed to invite a friend over, for fear of being labeled 'poor.' We were no longer poor!"[26] An executive director related a story of a new homeowner hugging everyone who entered his home on a wet, cold, and snowy dedication day, even the reporter, he was so excited.[27] Another homeowner says, "We are able to be part of a community and give something back to our community. And our new house has enabled us to be a real family. We don't just exist; we live!"[28] Still another homeowner celebrates her metamorphosis, "I didn't just receive a clean, healthy, and beautiful home; I received a new me!"[29]

Habitat's emphasis on the American Dream of owning a home is one reason it has been successful. As one executive director put it, "Culturally I grew up wanting my own home, part of the American Dream. Many immigrant groups want the same thing—everyone wants a yard, and the fence, their own space."[30] The belief is that not only will Habitat homeowners get a piece of the pie but they will also in turn become upstanding citizens and neighbors. This same executive director said that many of the immigrant families are shy and withdrawn at first, but after a year of classes on everything from home maintenance to financial basics, there is a physical transformation in their level of confidence and pride. Commenting on a political conversation she had with an El Salvadorean Habitat homeowner, this executive director said, "She was engaged in American politics, is in the community working hard, pays taxes. This is what you want, what you hope for."[31] The assumption is that these families became empowered individually and politically through the Habitat homeownership process.

Despite Habitat's faith in homeownership, most executive directors I spoke to felt that, while everyone should have the opportunity of homeownership, it is not in everyone's best interest. They argued that people must be ready to own a home, as homeownership entails a great deal of responsibility and can be burdensome. Furthermore, buying a home can limit mobility, which can be problematic for those with unstable jobs. One director noted that the stress of losing a home to foreclosure or disrepair can be devastating. Another director said, "Some people are better in their current situation [e.g., government-subsidized housing] because if they tried to own a home they might be underwater in a year."[32] Last of all, homeownership takes a certain amount of income, which many do not have. While most executive directors saw a need for more affordable rental housing, they felt Habitat should stick to its mission of offering low-income homeownership, as "any organization that tries to do too much won't be successful."[33]

Ideal Family and Home

Although not all staff at Habitat buys into Fuller's view of the ideal family and home, the foundation he laid still influences the philosophy of Habitat. The value of family is central to Habitat's understanding of healthy, empowered homeowners. The Habitat for Humanity Web site "Faces and Places—Homeowner Stories" includes many titles emphasizing family: "Home is a 'Happy Family'"; "The Healing of a Family"; "An Investment in Families"; and "The Restoration of a Family."[34] A majority of the stories Fuller cites are of nuclear families, although today many Habitat homeowners are single heads of household.

In extolling the health benefits of homeownership, Fuller writes, "Many things go together—husband and wife, open and honest, sweetness and light, neat and clean, robust and healthy. Good housing and good health also go together. They are entirely complementary."[35] Fuller explicitly claims owning a home makes cleanliness possible, and implicitly equates nuclear families of husband and wife with the virtues of cleanliness and healthiness.

Thus, the homeowners are pure and clean, and the home is a place where love and peace reign, and children are nurtured and supported: "A house is something visible. It is a place in which to be. An address—in a neighborhood. It is the site where loved ones live. It is where children study, play, and grow. It is where friends and family come to visit."[36] Former Habitat for Humanity CEO Paul Leonard referred to the home as a "place of rest and renewal from our day's labor and a safe harbor for moms, dads, and children."[37] On Habitat's Web site, a feature song by Anna Wilson titled "A House, A Home" is played: "Brick by brick, stone by stone / we build a place to call our own. / Going to fill it up with laughter . . . / joy and pride of seeing a house become a home, / a brighter future one family at a time."[38] While there are many stories of healthy families in Habitat homes, not all of them are. One homeowner in a sixteen-home Habitat development said, "Some families fight, and the police are here often."[39] Another said of her Habitat neighbor, "The house next door is a nightmare."[40]

Fuller holds that ideally Habitat affiliates will do "cluster building" of several Habitat houses together, creating a healthy community where each homeowner loves their home and keeps it up. Fuller contrasts this vision of a "neat and tidy" neighborhood with the "self-destructing" large-unit public housing projects.[41] Fuller claims that what sets Habitat families apart from other low-income families is that they were *chosen* to have a Habitat house. He goes on to say that "Habitat homeowners are *literally* a chosen people" just as the "children of Israel" were called to be "God's chosen people."[42] One executive director said that Habitat homes are for deserving people who are trying to make something for their families and just need a little help.[43]

To make sure each family can meet financial and cultural expectations to succeed as homeowners, each affiliate has "family nurturing committees." Fuller is aware that a good house is not a "panacea for everything," and therefore good family characteristics are crucial. He writes, "We don't just build houses, place families in them, and walk away. Our intention is to help the families succeed as homeowners."[44]

On the one hand, these committees can be a testimony to service and grace. One executive director shared the story of ten families that had participated on a build for a Vietnamese family, banding together to help this family when the father was paralyzed in a car accident. The committee members helped the mother get a job, tutored her in English, expedited disability payments with the help of lawyers, babysat their four children, and helped them restructure their mortgage.[45] On the other hand, these committees can be patronizing. Another executive director talked about "reading the riot act" to a female head of household who had not kept her new Habitat home clean, concluding that he should have kept her out of the program until she was better educated or had changed her ways.[46]

Habitat affiliates pick families based on need, ability to pay off their loan, and willingness to partner and do sweat-equity hours. The first two criteria are fairly objective, whereas the third criterion of willingness to partner is more subjective. Affiliate committees have large debates over which families will be "successful" partners from their point of view.[47] Sociologist of religion Jerome Baggett says that historically Habitat committees have had a subjective preference for "traditional" families, that is, two-parent, heterosexual families.[48]

Of the affiliates I visited, there were a number of female-headed households served, although some directors noted that alternative financing options (to the common fifteen-year loan) sometimes had to be considered for these families to afford house payments.[49] If there was any preference, it was toward families with children; as one director said, "We usually pick families with children over couples because of the impact having a house can have on children."[50] A Habitat couple without children (but a severe disability) said of the application meeting, "We didn't think we had a hope in hell because it is about families with children and the room was full of children."[51] While Habitat staff aim to treat all people with respect, and claim not to be in the "business of deciding who is worthy,"[52] they nevertheless are influenced by images of the ideal family and home.

A Hand Up, Not a Handout

Habitat's emphasis on transforming families stems in part from its belief that poverty is due to a cycle of dependency that is passed down through the generations. Habitat does identify external factors for poverty as well, such as unequal access to assets, lack of social capital, natural disasters and unexpected events, and oppression.[53] Their emphasis on independence, however, is what prompts both the partnership model and their concept of "sweat equity," where homeowners have to log five hundred hours of work toward homeownership. Original visionary for Habitat Clarence Jordan always claimed that the poor need "co-workers not caseworkers, capital not charity."[54] Hence, the Habitat phrase "a hand up, not a handout."[55]

President Jimmy Carter, who has sponsored an annual weeklong Carter work project for Habitat since 1984, is an advocate of the partnership ideal:

> Another thing I like about Habitat is that it's not a handout. We don't embarrass people by saying, "I'm a rich person, and I'm going to give you poor folks something for yourselves." Instead it's a partnership. It's not somebody up here helping somebody down there. It's somebody reaching out a hand and saying, "Let's work together."[56]

One executive director notes the importance of language: "We intentionally use the language of 'partners.' We never call what we do charity."[57] Former Habitat CEO Paul Leonard writes,

Habitat's approach was not the most efficient way to build an affordable house. But it was and is the best and most powerful way to build
dignity for its families and to create a community by bridging the
social and economic divide that cuts across our world. . . . Habitat for
Humanity does more than build houses.[58]

Habitat holds that families achieve dignity and pride precisely because
they purchase their homes, and because they contribute their own
labor. One homeowner said, "I know my house well as I literally helped
build it. I'm proud of this."[59]

Partnership entails people working together in community, what
Fuller called the "theology of the hammer," where people who might
disagree theologically or politically can agree on the idea of building
houses for God's people in need.[60] One executive director said that the
homeowners are conscious that faith motivates many of the volunteers, and in her experience, most families are very committed to giving
back to Habitat after they get a house.[61] Habitat argues that it is not
simply the rich that contribute. Volunteer Tom Hall writes, "The poor
are encouraged to give as they can. They are encouraged to contribute
their labor, their time and any extra material resources that they may
be able to obtain."[62] One homeowner who regularly volunteers, even
after having been in her house for two years, said, "I never thought to
volunteer before. I didn't realize how important it is."[63] She also noted,
however, that of all the Habitat families in her city, only two of them
volunteered with Habitat after fulfilling their sweat-equity hours and
getting a house. Yet, by regularly making their house payments to the
Fund for Humanity, Habitat homeowners are contributing toward the
construction of houses for other families. Fuller claimed that every payment is a religious act, an expression of Christian love.[64]

For Habitat, the concept of partnership is religious: "It's a partnership with God Almighty in heaven and it's a partnership with our
brothers and sisters on earth."[65] From partnership with God extends a
"whole network of partnerships."[66] Thus, the Habitat concept of partnership entails relationships and is especially about bringing the "affluent and the needy into a common effort of newness for both."[67] To build
the kingdom of God, relationships of love and care must be developed.

Every person must reach out to help others, and families who live in a decent house have a special responsibility to be part of the process of "passing it on."[68] Partnering with God multiplies human effort, and "Habitat's unimaginable goal becomes, through the eyes of faith, suddenly imaginable."[69]

Baggett notes that one reason for the organization's popularity is the sweat-equity requirement marking the homeowners as "deserving poor" who are not just trying to get something for nothing.[70] As one volunteer notes, "I love Habitat's premise. The sweat equity, the fact that the family is able to work for this instead of just being given something. I can't imagine how they must feel!"[71] Baggett offers a quote from a Habitat assistant regional director:

> We have a tendency to sell Habitat by announcing that we have a family selection process by which we pick good people who are willing to work on their house for five hundred hours. So we tell people that these families deserve a break because they have what it takes to be like us and they're not going to screw up the neighborhood.[72]

Many of the homeowner stories on Habitat's Web site highlight the hard work, initiative, and sacrifice of Habitat families. For example, Virginia Burden worked full-time as a nurse's assistant for years until her daughter died in a car accident, leaving Virginia with three grandchildren to raise.[73] Another story talks about a family's sacrifice:

> When Jason and Casey Burt committed themselves to doing whatever it would take to have a home for their growing family, they were prepared to make the sacrifice—and they did. They moved into a truck-top camper in the yard of Jason's parents for more than a year to save money, piecing together sleeping space for their children, then 6 months, 18 months and 4 years, out of a playpen, cushions and a small bunk bed.[74]

Still another family made improvements on their rental property for a discount in rent, only to have the landlord sell the place to someone else.[75]

Many Habitat supporters, both conservative and liberal alike, believe that Habitat empowers individuals, while the state fosters dependency. In other words, subsidized rental housing keeps people passive, while having title to a home gives them initiative.[76] CEO Jonathan Reckford cites a story of two Argentinian families who lived on similar-sized lots and had similar incomes, showing that the family that had title to its home exhibited much more entrepreneurial spirit and hard work than the family that did not have title.[77] Thus, he argues, property rights are central to empowerment. Presumably, when people *own* their housing, they will have more of a stake in the upkeep of their property, their neighborhoods, and the larger community. In one homeowner testimony, Rhonda Reese says, "Owning something of your own just makes you want to work harder."[78]

Reckford advocates a level playing field of equal opportunity for all to achieve the American Dream of homeownership and success, yet he does not think society should ensure more than a minimum basic standard of living. He believes equal opportunity can be achieved in a free market economy with voluntary stewardship and charity. He says, "Habitat's philosophy is about opportunity rather than entitlement." Reckford argues that, without a free market, people cannot gain any assets, yet he also holds that poverty and barriers to equal opportunity must be addressed. While he argues for Martin Luther King's "beloved community," he claims it is not a place but a "state of heart and mind, a spirit of hope and goodwill that transcends all boundaries and barriers and embraces all creation." In his view, poverty will be addressed when people with power take practical steps out of care and compassion to ensure equal opportunity for all, but then it will be up to people without as much power to take advantage of the opportunities offered.[79]

Changing the Consciousness of the Rich

Habitat claims that the way to eliminate poverty housing in the world is by making that challenge a matter of conscience.[80] Fuller talks about opulent homes and the hoarding of wealth, but says the solution is to "break into the consciousness of the rich" and change their perspective,

and not, as some might argue, to change the structures that create vast
inequality. President Carter puts this emphasis on individual conscience
well:

> Plant projects all over the world; sow seeds of hope, encouraging the
> poor to do all they can to help themselves; and cultivate consciences
> among the affluent, urging them, privately or corporately, to join
> less fortunate folks in a spirit of partnerships, to solve the problem
> together.[81]

Habitat is a ministry not only to those in need but also to the affluent,
who, Fuller argues, need to probe deeply into their spiritual souls and
open up to the healing hand of God. In doing so, he hopes that just as
he did, they will begin to use their God-given gifts for the promotion of
God's kingdom rather than self-interest.[82]

Fuller decries the conservative, salvation-oriented Christianity
that he grew up with that did not connect being Christian with seeking
justice. He argues that believing in Jesus should be more than a verbal
commitment. Thus, Habitat emphasizes the practical steps of doing the
ministry of Jesus. A favorite Clarence Jordan quotation of one executive
director is, "The Baptists worship the hind legs off Jesus, but just won't
do what he says."[83] For Fuller, true religion is about more than worship;
action is required. He does not think we can be disciples of Jesus if we
live in affluence while there are people "who do not have a decent place
to live, or a good roof over their heads, or a solid floor under their feet,
or insulation in their walls," and we are doing nothing to alleviate these
conditions.[84] Jordan felt that the rich simply need "a wise, honorable
and just way of divesting themselves of their overabundance."[85] Habitat
for Humanity offers a practical Christian mission that binds the opu-
lence of the wealthy to the suffering of the poor.

Fuller does not think that doing good works brings salvation, as he
holds salvation is a free gift from God, but he does advocate a "life of
giving back" as an expression of gratitude to God. David Rowe, former
president of Habitat International's board of directors, put it this way:
"We don't build so that we can get into heaven. If you think so, leave
now. We build because heaven is a glimpse of God's love. Our building is

a symbol of how God's love and our love can work together."[86] All people are made in the image of God, and God wants "*all* of His people to share in the good things in life."[87] If people would stop using their talents for self-interest and instead heed the powerful voice of Isaiah and become disciples of Jesus, there would not be millions of people languishing in misery. God expects us to share from our abundance, and we do so out of thankfulness for the blessings we have received from God.

Jonathan Reckford talks about his experience of "holy discontent" on a mission trip to India where he worked with the Bhangi Dalits, who live in abject poverty. He called his discontent "holy" because it gave him a sense of urgency to respond. His hope is that as people reach out and serve as "God's hands, heart, and instruments of love," more people will be filled with holy discontent, motivating them not only to build more houses but also to advocate against poverty and substandard housing.[88] Habitat claims that their volunteers learn what it means to be disciples of Christ—to promote justice, live simply, and serve others. Habitat's new emphasis on building green also teaches volunteers about environmental sustainability. Furthermore, Habitat's practice of each affiliate tithing 10 percent of its cash donations to Habitat International for new houses overseas is a way to model redistribution of wealth.

Building Communities of Commonality

In addition to building simple, decent homes for people, Habitat also seeks to bring about the beloved community where peace reigns and people look out for one another. One of Habitat's mission principles is, "Engage broad community through inclusive leadership and diverse partnerships."[89] Builds are a place for a diversity of people to come together around a common cause of constructing homes, and Habitat claims people will come to recognize their commonalities as a result of working together. One Habitat volunteer writes, "And no matter one's race or creed, politics or other persuasion, the ground on which Habitat partners find commonality is a haven for unity—a fertile field for compassion and true reconciliation."[90]

Fuller's "theology of the hammer" is the most fully developed explanation of Habitat's goal of building communities of commonality. Fuller emphasizes Jesus' ministry of bringing good news to the poor and Jesus' admonishments to the rich to share all they had with those who have little. Sharing "possessions, time, and ideas with the poor is clear. It is not an option. It is a requirement."[91] All that exists is God's, given to us as a gift, and so we should share our gifts and talents and not hoard material things to ourselves. Healthy communities will exist when we *all* can flourish, and it is a responsibility of Christians to partner with God in creating such communities. The hammer is "an instrument to manifest God's love," a way for us to come together despite our differences and build communities of commonality.[92]

In light of Habitat's mission to build communities of commonality, a number of affiliates have organized interfaith builds (often with volunteers from Christian, Jewish, or Muslim faith traditions). Affiliates also have tried to involve church communities from different racial and ethnic communities, but some affiliates have been less successful at getting minority congregations involved on a regular basis, even if they have individual minority volunteers at builds and on Habitat committees and boards.[93] Habitat does not collect national demographic information on staff and boards of directors, as each affiliate is independently run. Based on observations, all of the leadership at the five affiliates I visited was white. Two of the five executive directors I interviewed were female, and there were plenty of female staff at the larger affiliates I examined.

Habitat recognizes that part of building a beloved community involves not simply building affordable housing but also advocating for policies that promote affordable and decent housing. Thus, another of its mission principles is, "Advocate on behalf of those in need of decent shelter," which entails working "to eliminate restraints that contribute to poverty and poverty housing."[94] Several of the affiliates I visited had staff on county committees to address homelessness and to provide low-income housing, while others acted independently and were not involved in any advocacy efforts. An adapted version of a report on advocacy submitted to the Habitat International board of directors in late 2005 is found in Habitat's publication *Kingdom Building for the*

21st Century. This piece is long on generalities of how the Christian faith and prophetic tradition calls us to advocate but short on details of what type of policies we should be advocating for.[95] Apart from this document, I found very little Habitat literature written about advocacy.

Conclusion

The philosophical and theological foundations for Habitat's work have been well articulated over the years by Millard Fuller, with inspiration from Clarence Jordan. Since 2005, Habitat has had new leadership and direction, yet the themes that inspired the organization and helped it to grow are still prevalent. Clearly, not all congregations or individual volunteers who work with Habitat are going to agree with all of the Habitat themes, nor will all congregations who are involved with the strategy of creating affordable housing, especially if they are focusing on rental housing. Nevertheless, since some of these themes do emerge in low-income housing approaches with which churches are involved, it is worthwhile identifying them for critical analysis. Habitat's emphasis on homeownership and giving a hand up and not a handout are features that make the program popular with many Americans. There can be benefits to homeownership, especially accruing equity and creating stability, that make this emphasis attractive. Furthermore, contributing to make their homeownership a reality can bring a certain dignity and feeling of accomplishment to Habitat homeowners.

Habitat's emphasis on the ideal family and home is perhaps less overt today than it was in Fuller's writings but is nevertheless a theme that exists, albeit unconsciously. Habitat still places great emphasis on partnerships that lead to communities of commonality and partnerships that change the consciousness of the rich. Although they give a nod to advocacy in support of changing public policies, they generally limit their focus to transforming people through relationships and serving as a private alternative for addressing low-income housing. While limited in how extensively they can address the lack of affordable housing, they are doing an admirable job of taking action and serving as "God's hands, heart, and instruments of love."

Discussion Questions

1. Has your faith community been involved in promoting opportunities for low-income homeownership (or low-income rentals)? Share stories of your experiences with this approach.

2. While there are benefits to homeownership, what are the positive and negative implications of emphasizing homeownership as transformative? How does uplifting homeownership help the homeless?

3. What are the positive and negative implications of emphasizing a hand up, not a handout, and partnership rather than charity?

4. What are the positive and negative implications of addressing homelessness and substandard housing by changing the consciousness of the rich, by asking them to use their God-given gifts for the promotion of God's kingdom rather than self-interest?

5. How can faith communities build communities of commonality that encourage true diversity and participation? Can congregations and church organizations provide affordable housing alone or are public-policy changes and larger government support necessary?

−6−

Prophetic-Disruption Assessment
and Response

A Christian ethical response to homelessness based on a methodology of prophetic disruption would support charitable programs and private initiatives toward homeownership as legitimate ways of showing Christian love and support for people in poverty but would not view these approaches alone as sufficient. AGRM's shelters do not solve the long-term housing needs of the homeless. And as impressive as Habitat's efforts have been, the 200,000 homes they have built worldwide hardly make a dent in the 3.5 million people without a home in the United States, let alone the rest of the world.[1] Nor are the very poor served, as many people do not make enough to make payments on a home loan.

A prophetic disruption method also would lead us to examine both the ways in which these approaches are liberating and the ways in which they adopt or leave intact dominant views on housing and homelessness that do not prophetically disrupt the status quo by challenging inequality and oppression. To make this assessment, attention to the literature and the practice of each organization, as well as to the stories of the people most affected, will be important.

I began employing Traci West's ethical methodology earlier in the book when I identified the dominant ideologies on homelessness and housing. Throughout her work, West identifies dominant ideologies and myths and shows how they are actualized through institutional response. In fact, the four myths I identify in chapter 2 about people who are homeless—that they are unreliable, incompetent, and mentally unstable; are homeless because of a personal fault or characteristic; choose to be homeless; and need discipline and structure to put order in their lives—are based on the popularly held beliefs society constructs about black women, which West discusses in her work. For both the homeless and black women, these constructions legitimate violence against them and invalidate their experiences of victimization.

In this chapter, I will use West's liberationist ethical method to analyze critically the responses illustrated by AGRM and Habitat for Humanity. I will begin by noting the ways in which these types of response can be empowering, or at least helpful, for the people served. Both aim to help people out of poverty: AGRM by helping people overcome drug or alcohol addictions, Habitat by helping people become homeowners. Then I will examine how these responses fall short in addressing homelessness and inadequate housing and can even contribute to the problems. Neither of these responses challenges the status quo of privilege and power, and in fact, by adopting dominant ideologies about homelessness and housing, they actually support the status quo. My intention is not to disregard or dismiss the important role that these agencies play in addressing certain aspects of homelessness. My intention is to help Christian communities see the inadequacy of private approaches that focus on individual transformation and do not address structural changes in society. If we are truly to make a home for all in God's just and compassionate community, we will need to challenge and disrupt the dominant ideologies that support the current inequitable power structure and advocate for antipoverty policies that address the root causes of homelessness and inadequate housing.

Empowering Aspects of Models

What staff at rescue mission affiliates do best is journey with people in their troubles. A substantial number (although not the majority) of staff were formerly homeless and thus know what it is like to deal with poverty and know the barriers to housing. From my observations, most of the staff at mission affiliates treat the guests with dignity. The affiliates that go the extra mile to beautify their buildings show even more respect to those they serve. Offering addiction programs for people who have no money to pay for them is a needed service in our society. Addressing spiritual as well as physical needs for people with addictions can be positive for many, especially if the worth and dignity of each person and the presence of a compassionate God are affirmed. Less empowering is an emphasis on sinfulness and a punishing God that some affiliates profess.

Offering overnight shelters for single men (a majority of missions do not have overnight shelters for single women) and extended shelters and transitional housing for families is also important in a society with as much homelessness as ours. What AGRM needs to be commended for for the most is their presence with people in poverty and their good-faith efforts in preparing homeless and marginalized people to survive in a country that has deemed them expendable. Working directly with people who are homeless can show Christian love and hospitality so long as we accord full dignity to all people and do not see ourselves as the saviors of the morally lost. The goal, however, should always be to prevent homelessness, not simply to develop more and more "houses of hospitality." That is, we should work at treating the causes rather than the symptoms.

What Habitat does best is offer the option of homeownership to people who are stable and responsible yet unable to afford market-rate house payments and interest on a loan. Habitat has done a good job of narrowing their focus to one segment of the low-income population and one area of housing. For those families who are lucky enough to get picked as Habitat homeowners, the experience appears to be empowering. Most Habitat homeowners stay in their houses for a substantial period of time, leading to equity in their homes and stability in their neighborhoods.[2]

Habitat's philosophy of no-interest loans is refreshing in an age of predatory lending and unscrupulous subprime loans with ballooning payments. Its biblically based practice of tithing 10 percent from each affiliate to support houses in developing countries is a model of redistribution of wealth that our nation might emulate. (Currently in the United States only 1 percent of the national budget is put toward development aid, and much more is taken from poor countries for interest payments on debt.) Furthermore, its insistence on simple housing and increasing support of "green" housing is an antidote to the millions of unsustainable megahomes that developers are building in response to consumer demand. Last, its understanding of partnership, where the less-well-off and the better-off both contribute to a beloved society, is commendable. Creating opportunities for homeownership is also a way to practice Christian love, and works to address one of the key causes of homelessness, lack of affordable housing.

Blaming the Undeserving Homeless

When I teach a college social justice course, I require all students to do fifteen hours of service with an organization that works with low-income people. Without a deeper understanding of structural causes of poverty to help them reflect critically on their service experience, many students can have stereotypical beliefs about poverty and people in poverty reinforced. Sociologist Herbert Gans says that Americans commonly assume that "most behavior is caused by the holding and practicing of values." In other words, we think that good behavior is a result of good values and bad behavior of bad ones, without recognizing the "economic, political, and other structural conditions to which people must react."[3] Although staffpersons at rescue missions are often aware of the structural conditions with which people in poverty struggle and the scarcity of options available to them, the overarching belief is that the predicament they are in is a result of bad values that caused them to make bad choices. While most staff believe that all people are deserving of help since everyone is a child of God, only those guests who are willing to be changed are deemed worthy of entering their addiction programs. That is, if they are willing to abandon their bad values and adopt Jesus as Christ and Savior, then supposedly their bad behavior will also change.

The assumption that something is wrong with the individual is extended to all homeless people, not just people who suffer addictions. As Stephen Burger has said, the homeless person's "fundamental way of thinking" must be challenged. Many staff members assume that people are homeless primarily due to bad choices, whether the choice was to become addicted to alcohol and/or drugs, to pick an abusive partner, or to have more children than one is able to support. This worldview is so insidious that even when most staff members hear stories of structural obstacles from guests, they still interpret the choices as freely made apart from the constraints and environmental pressures of poverty.

By not acknowledging the systemic and structural obstacles people in poverty face, AGRM can invalidate the victimization that they experience. Attributing the cause of homelessness to individual spiritual shortcomings with no attention to economic factors further victimizes them. It is no coincidence that every female client I interviewed at women's shelters and in transitional housing grew up with poverty and abuse. Listening to their stories makes one aware how they have been victimized throughout their lives, but also of how they have continued to have agency and have resisted their victimization. For example, one woman left home early to get away from parents who were heroin addicts. Although she also became addicted to drugs, she recounted stories of her resourcefulness in getting by on her own at age fifteen, as well as stories of helping others find resources for survival.[4]

While the stories of the victimization and resourcefulness of people on the margins should be morally central, different conclusions about homelessness could be drawn from such stories. One could infer from the previous story that this woman's behavior was a result of bad values and a learned "culture of poverty." Alternatively, one could conclude that leaving her parents to live on the streets was a rational choice and that her heroin addiction was a result of various environmental factors that have less to do with a learned culture and bad values and more to do with oppression, abuse, and poverty. Clearly, not all of her choices were influenced by bad values, and she managed to survive and even help others despite limited options. Unfortunately, many will only see that she ended up a homeless addict and will never take the time to hear her story and the reasons behind her "choices."

We need to acknowledge simultaneously victimization as well as agency. People dealing with poverty and homelessness make choices every day. We should neither view them as incapable of rational choices nor treat them as children. If we understand the structural constraints people face, we will be less likely to view their choices as irrational. We spend an inordinate amount of time dissecting and condemning people's choices and very little on the structural factors that influence and constrain their options.

Since AGRM staff tends to see more people who are chronically homeless than episodically or situationally homeless, it is understandable why they think the majority of people are homeless due to addictions and/or mental illness. While addictions and mental illness are disproportionately found in the ranks of the homeless, there is a large number of homeless people for whom this is not the case and plenty of people with addictions and mental illness who are housed. Attributing these causes to everyone without a home turns the concept of "homeless" into a prejudicial label rather than a description of one's situation. The term originally denoted being without a home but has now become a way to label derogatorily a group of people, just as in the past these people were called vagrant, hobo, and beggar. Labels are based on stereotypes, not on the real experiences of actual people.

AGRM plays into this labeling by both assuming that the "homeless" are a homogenous group of people with sinful behavior and by ignoring the various structural causes of homelessness. Their brochures that claim the homeless are "friendless" and "unlovable" further support the negative image. The effect of such labeling is that being homeless becomes equated with being bad and undeserving. We do not even need to listen to the stories of people who are homeless because we can simply assume that they are "lying in the bed that they made." The "homeless" label also gets used as a racial code word, allowing society to conveniently cover antiblack or anti-Latino sentiments.

Herbert Gans outlines several harmful ramifications of negative labeling. First, labels can cause institutions and individuals to pursue punitive actions. Focusing on behavior hides the poverty that creates the behavior, and therefore individuals can be blamed and punished for their bad choices and society gets off scot-free from having to address poverty and oppression. Gans points out that in most communities it is easier to get drugs and alcohol than low-income housing; yet we continue to put taxpayer money toward prison construction over affordable housing. Second, if we hold that bad behavior causes homelessness, we simply need to transform individuals, not structures and policy. AGRM focuses on helping its guests jump from a culture of poverty to middle-class culture but does not advocate for such things as living-wage jobs with benefits, universal healthcare, or excellent inner-city schools.[5]

Third, negative labels can lead to depression and demoralization in those who are labeled, often resulting in self-fulfilling prophecies, especially in children. When parents are labeled, it is more likely that their kids will be branded as well, subjecting them to punitive actions in school and society, often apart from any behavior they exhibit. For example, some teachers may have lower academic expectations of students who are known to be from broken homes. Fourth, labeling results in fewer services for people who are labeled. For example, the decrease in welfare benefits in 1996 was justified by negatively labeling welfare moms and picturing them as black (despite more white women on welfare at the time). Some poor people will not even seek help because of their experiences of negative treatment and inferior service based on their status.[6]

While lumping all the homeless into one group can lead to labeling, making distinctions among different types of homeless people can also promote labeling, especially between the so-called "deserving" and "undeserving" homeless. For example, families with a working parent and small children might be seen as deserving, while an addict who has never held a job in the formal sector would be considered undeserving. On the one hand, it is necessary to distinguish the reasons people are homeless to determine what type of assistance they might need (e.g., child care, addiction program, mental health care). On the other hand, if we had antipoverty policies in place, there would be considerably less homelessness, and people could be treated for addictions or mental health without the added stigma of being "homeless."

Labeling is often done unconsciously. While some AGRM staff overtly labeled the homeless negatively, most did not. Yet, the emphasis on changing what is wrong in individuals without addressing what is wrong in society places all the blame on "deviant individuals." An approach of prophetic disruption would challenge the ideologies that people are homeless simply because of bad choices, that people choose to be homeless, and that with adequate discipline people will overcome poverty. We should not spend too much time disproving stereotypes, however, for this would be to accept the assumption that the problem is within those who are homeless. It would be more productive to identify and address the structural obstacles people struggle with, especially the majority of the homeless who face episodic and situational homelessness.

People who have experienced poverty and/or homelessness know what the structural obstacles are. More often than not, their insights are not sought out, however. When they are able to share their perspectives, they are not always heard, as listeners assimilate information through a lens that emphasizes individual agency over structural factors and constraints. If we could stop labeling the homeless and realize that most of them are like the majority of working-class Americans who are just trying to get by in a political economy of vast inequality, we could build a movement with them to alleviate poverty and open up our democracy to meaningful participation for all.

An approach of prophetic disruption would also examine how racism is connected to poverty and homelessness. Although AGRM serves large numbers of people of color, it does not do any sort of racial analysis of poverty and homelessness. Nor does it do any racial analysis of how its organization provides services (apart from identifying the demographics of people served); the demographics of its employees or volunteers versus its clients; or how its organization mirrors or challenges societal assumptions on race. Race analysis is crucial to avoid reinforcing oppressive ideologies and practices. For example, the emphasis on individual deficiencies, dependency, and a lack of discipline as the main causes of homelessness is closely related to negative racial stereotypes made of many people of color. The solution then becomes changing people of color instead of challenging practices and structures that create poverty and homelessness. The result is that the "we" who have power (mostly white) aim to change the "them" (overwhelmingly minority), instead of identifying as part of the problem our society that still gives greater advantages to whites.[7]

Similarly, an approach of prophetic disruption would be wary of organizations that uphold a conservative understanding of women's roles and fail to have an in-depth analysis of the ways that oppression of women and non-heterosexuals is connected to poverty and homelessness. An emphasis on traditional gender roles can be especially difficult for women who feel that they have failed at motherhood and even can be dangerous for women who are homeless as a result of domestic abuse. Assuming everyone must fit the mold of heterosexuality alienates people with a different sexual orientation and can also be dangerous, as the higher rate of gay and lesbian homeless youth attests.[8] While West's ethical method is open to a plurality of theological perspectives, it challenges theological interpretations that support domination and oppression.

Uplifting the Deserving Homeowner

Since Habitat does not address homelessness directly, most staff and volunteers would probably not consider themselves in the practice of negatively labeling people who are homeless. Yet some of Habitat's themes, in particular its vision of ideal homeowners, its emphasis on individual transformation, and its effort to reward a deserving poor, indirectly label. Furthermore, its emphasis on the democratic ideal of partnership without addressing asymmetry of power between volunteers and homeowners serves to mask oppressive realities that ushered in the need for a program like Habitat for Humanity in the first place.

Placing homeownership on such a high pedestal, as Habitat for Humanity does, can be disempowering for those who do not reach this expectation, or who do, but find its benefits elusive. Many studies have shown the benefits of homeownership, some of which are justifiably important (e.g., financial equity, stability for children, and pride of ownership). It is not always clear, however, whether homeownership leads to positive behaviors or whether owners were already predisposed to such behavior. Either way, the home is a symbol for Habitat of all that is normal, good, and respectable (and ideally the normal and good family in the home is a heterosexual, middle-class nuclear family). Thus, the goal for Habitat is to transform families so they may reach this norm.

While there is validity in having communities in which there are stable homeowners who participate as leaders in their communities, a prophetic-disruption approach would challenge the white, middle-class ethos that pervades the normative Habitat homeowner image. As long as staff and volunteers are primarily white, able-bodied, and middle class, it will be more difficult for Habitat to change this worldview. For example, a Russian homeowner's concern about enough land to grow crops was not taken seriously by one affiliate, as it assumed a family would work in the formal sector and buy its food.[9] Another family with one member who was paraplegic had to exert exceptional effort to modify Habitat house plans.[10] Listening to the homeowners and incorporating their understanding of family and citizenship into the mix would begin to challenge the idea that somehow their understandings are lacking. As long as there is such a heavy emphasis on transformation of families after homeownership, there will always be the assumption that somehow families were culturally lacking before becoming Habitat homeowners.

While Millard Fuller clearly had traditional ideas about gender roles in the household, it is not clear that Habitat for Humanity as an organization consciously promotes such roles. In contrast to traditional gender roles, they expect all of their single-mother homeowners to have a job in order to pay their mortgages. Nevertheless, its image of the ideal homeowner plays into the Christian Right's promotion of "family values." Despite Habitat's clear standards against any form of discrimination, it would be interesting to know if there are many openly identified same-sex couples in Habitat homes.

An approach of prophetic disruption would also critique the ideology that ownership of private property in the form of a home will bring about miracle transformations within individuals and families. Recent studies have shown that even if a family can get a loan to buy a home, this does not ensure financial stability and prosperity. Homeowners still must be able to pay insurance, property taxes, and maintenance costs. Homeowner's insurance rose 62 percent from 1995 to 2005. Low-income homeowners often have high insurance costs due to poor or limited credit. Between 1997 and 2002, property tax rates rose by 19 percent, with ten states having property tax increases of 30 percent or more.[11] Many low-income homeowners are in unstable jobs with stagnant incomes. Unexpected events can cause home loss. From 1976 to 1993, 36 percent of low-income households gave up or lost their homes within two years and 53 percent within five years.[12]

While current nationwide data on tenure of low-income households does not exist,[13] the recent mortgage foreclosure crisis has disproportionately affected low-income households.[14] Subprime loans were encouraged as a way for struggling working-class families with bad credit histories to become, as former President George W. Bush said, "stakeholders" in an "Ownership Society."[15] Despite Bush's claim, only 11 percent of subprime loans went to first-time homebuyers. Most subprime loans were refinancing loans to pay for other expenses. Many black and Latino borrowers were pressured to take out subprime loans, even though over 55 percent of subprime borrowers had credit scores high enough for a conventional mortgage.[16] While Habitat ensures that families will not have risky loans, and they work with families to restructure their mortgages if necessary, it is not clear that families are instantly transformed simply by owning a home.

By equating homeownership with success and placing such an emphasis on "willingness to work" toward success, Habitat buys into our society's judgment of people who appear to be "dependent" and are not making it on their own and furthers the distinction between the deserving and undeserving poor. In fact, the upper middle class and rich get most of the federal housing aid, but rarely are they considered dependent or undeserving. Similarly, Habitat volunteers are considered empowered and spiritually enriched simply by showing up to help on a build, whereas Habitat homeowners are only considered so if they show that they have adopted the middle-class homeowner ethos of cleanliness, responsibility, and civic-mindedness, and have proven their work ethic through sweat-equity hours.

On the one hand, the concept of sweat equity is a way for Habitat homeowners to participate, have a vested interest in their home, and feel pride in their achievement. On the other hand, the better-off never have to work extra hours in addition to their full-time job and family life to be considered worthy of owning a home. Does this requirement assume that people in poverty are not working hard enough? Five hundred sweat-equity hours translates to over sixty-two eight-hour days, or one day each week for over a year, quite a feat for working single parents to complete. An approach of prophetic disruption would challenge a double standard that expects people in poverty to prove their worth. Again, contrary to popular belief, the lion's share of government subsidies and aid goes to the better-off, yet we rarely consider them unworthy.[17]

On the surface, Habitat's idea of partnership is attractive, as all should partner together to create a better society. Without identifying power inequities or naming the "normative" ethos of middle-class white volunteers, however, it is not clear, as sociologist Jerome Baggett points out, that all homeowners truly feel empowered as partners or whether they are simply following the rules for material gain.[18] Emphasizing egalitarian ideals in situations where there is asymmetry of power can obscure and hide realities of domination and oppression that exist in our society. Thus, Habitat volunteers and staff can feel that they empowered Habitat families without ever having to question the inequalities in power and privilege that support oppression and create families in need of empowerment.

Minimal Structural Critique

Using prophetic-disruption methodology entails not simply deconstructing oppressive ideologies but also identifying and addressing power, privilege, and social domination. In short, the method insists on power analysis of structures and practices. While the dualistic ideologies of undeserving homeless and deserving homeowner serve to justify oppressive realities and further practices of differential treatment, the root of the problem is an economic system that is premised on "survival of the fittest." Thus, we also must be aware of how we adopt ideologies that justify excessive wealth accumulation by a few at the expense of others who suffer extreme poverty and marginalization.

While both AGRM and Habitat for Humanity have programs that address structural issues, neither of them does much to disrupt and challenge oppressive policies and practices of institutions and our political economy that hinder people from being adequately housed. Some rescue missions have programs that seek to mentor and provide enriched educational opportunities for youth in poor communities (addresses structural issue of inadequate schools), and Habitat provides low-income housing for families in poverty (addresses structural issue of inadequate housing). Yet most of the philosophy and practices of AGRM and Habitat accommodates to substantial inequality of wealth and power in our society.

Habitat's emphasis on the "economics of Jesus" could be construed as a critique of our capitalist system, but without sustained critical analysis of aspects of the capitalist system that cause homelessness, substandard housing, and lack of affordable housing, Habitat home building simply becomes an alternative that fits quite nicely within the status quo.[19] Habitat's encouragement of corporate partnerships without a power analysis of the conservative political influence of corporations will probably keep the organization from adopting an ethics of disruption, especially as Habitat itself becomes more corporatelike in the way it is run.[20]

So long as Habitat emphasizes changing the conscience of the rich, it will not adopt a structural critique. Its focus is less on the power of structures and more on opportunities for caring, better-off individuals who are willing to give back some of what they have been "blessed" with.[21] An approach of prophetic disruption would critique our capitalist system and would be wary of simply offering alternatives without challenging the ways in which the system is oppressive. Furthermore, it would strategically challenge social and economic policies that marginalize and exploit people and would support policies that redistribute wealth and power more evenly. Simply persuading the rich to give up their wealth voluntarily is naïve and does not address unequal power relations. In fact, philanthropy keeps in place the power and privilege of the givers because they have sole prerogative on what gets funded, even as they are commended for their charity and good-heartedness.

Both AGRM and Habitat are more apt to critique state-fostered dependency and governmental provision of services than they are to critique corporate power. Thus, they can claim they transform individuals without ever addressing the ways in which corporate profit is made on the backs of the poor. Capitalist profit is achieved in part by keeping labor costs down and by maintaining a reserve of unemployed seeking work. Private nonprofit service agencies like AGRM and Habitat are in fact serving those who are negatively affected by this system, yet they never make a structural critique of it. Their distrust of the state and embrace of the private nonprofit sector that is addressing poverty goes along with their emphasis on individual transformation. The belief is that government will squelch the individual, whereas the private sector, especially voluntary organizations like AGRM and Habitat, will promote self-sufficiency and individual initiative. No assessment is made of the ways in which corporate power ensures that a segment of the population remains in poverty with limited options to exercise initiative.

In support of their own institutional advancement, these nonprofit organizations have often tended to portray themselves as more efficient, flexible, and personal than bureaucratic governmental agencies. Any large-scale institution can become bureaucratic, but preventing homelessness requires a multi-angle and large-scale approach. Nonprofit voluntary organizations should be part of the picture, but their work does not replace governmental action and antipoverty policies. By setting themselves apart from the state, nonprofit voluntary agencies feed into an antigovernment sentiment that fails to see the importance of a public approach to the common good.

The government is the only institution that can regulate excessive profit-making that exploits people and the environment. Further, it is the only institution that has the ability and the mandate to address basic societal welfare on a large scale and construct tax codes in ways that benefit the poor instead of the wealthy. The nonprofit voluntary sector is not equipped to prevent homelessness or to provide low-income housing on a large scale, and the corporate sector is primarily interested in endeavors that increase its bottom line (despite corporate giving).

Ironically, as nonprofit organizations aim to serve more people, they often accept government funding. Increasingly, Habitat affiliates are involved in public-private partnerships with HUD, especially in the HOPE VI programs of redeveloping public housing projects into mixed-income neighborhoods. Even some rescue missions that have steadfastly refused government funding in the past have accepted funding for overnight shelters, transitional housing, and soup kitchens. The increasing numbers of nonprofit and voluntary organizations contracted by the government—what Jennifer Wolch calls the "shadow state"—support the shift of responsibility for welfare to the private sector, even if private service activities are "enabled, regulated and subsidized by the state."[22] Wolch notes that with this privatization comes a loss of universalism where all are served according to need, not according to merit (e.g., deservingness).[23] Furthermore, she notes that in the past the nonprofit voluntary sector could neither adequately address the problems associated with poverty nor ameliorate entrenched inequality.

Becoming a More Compassionate Society

Making a place for all in God's compassionate community entails prophetically disrupting policies and practices that physically exploit and exclude particular people as well as the ideologies that justify such exploitation and exclusion. As West writes, "Hope for ethical relationships is only found in one's participation in the process of becoming a more compassionate society, in confronting the multiple patterns of denial, devaluation, and abuse or assaults."[24] Thus, the way in which we respond to people who are poor and/or homeless and the approaches we take for addressing the problem of homelessnes are just as important as any outcomes our actions bring about.

The first step in the process of becoming a more compassionate society is to start from the lived reality of those who are homeless and understand what obstacles thwart their ability to live flourishing lives. How different would Christian approaches that rescue the homeless and help them toward recovery or that create affordable housing look if we quit seeing the homeless as having the problems? How would such approaches look if we saw the gospel as less about individual relationship with Jesus Christ and more about the physical, spiritual, and mental health of people within God's community? Assuming that the spiritual crisis is within specific individuals alone without addressing the ways in which our society is spiritually impoverished simply blames those who are the victims of such a society.

We live in a society of substantial inequality, with neighborhoods, schools, and churches segregated by class and race. Those who live in wealthy communities do not encounter substandard housing, drug trafficking, violence, and a proliferation of liquor stores and predatory check-cashing shops but no grocery stores. There is also a substantial difference in quality between schools in white suburbs and poor neighborhoods that are predominantly of color. Better-off youth assume their successes are a result of their hard work and effort, not realizing that the deck has been stacked in their favor. Until we promote communities where all youth are given opportunities to flourish, we cannot blame people on the margins for their poverty and homelessness. An approach of prophetic disruption will listen to people who are homeless or close to homelessness and find out what obstacles, both personal and structural, they face.

Disrupting policies and ideologies that create barriers for flourishing lives and *advocating* for worldviews and policies that seek to include everyone in God's compassionate community are the second step of a prophetic response. Being involved in direct hospitality efforts is laudable, but we must not promote the ideologies that label people, and we should simultaneously be involved in advocating for social and economic policies that work to end poverty and oppression. Since no one individually can be involved in addressing all problems, a social movement is necessary. A social movement can include people from all walks of life but must be in solidarity with people who are marginalized and/or exploited. An approach of prophetic disruption claims that all church communities and Christians are called to participate in a social movement to create just and peaceful communities.

An approach of prophetic disruption holds that the multiple ways people are exploited and marginalized must be addressed simultaneously. For example, simply providing affordable housing without at the same time organizing for workers' rights, for equitable and excellent educational systems, or against institutional racism will not adequately support people to have flourishing lives. Congregations can each pick an area to address, while also working in coalitions across areas of concern and in solidarity with the people most negatively affected.

While money has considerable influence in our political system, we are still a democracy, and large coalitions can have political clout. Passage of women's right to vote, civil rights legislation, and disability rights are but three examples. More and more middle-class families are feeling the pinch with the economic recession. While there are multiple ways to respond to economic hard times, a prophetic-disruption approach argues against exclusive responses, that is, tactics that aim to protect what private property, wealth, and privilege one has by excluding and/or exploiting the "other." Christians and church communities are called instead to be in solidarity with the most exploited and marginalized by participating in a movement for social and economic justice.

Actively promoting such a movement will require courage to stand up to oppression and domination in its multiple forms and to weather the response to such resistance. It is always easier to deny complicity in oppressive systems if we have done individual good deeds and have not been overtly exclusionary. God, through the example of Jesus Christ, calls us to more, however. Jesus did not revel in his own purity at the expense of injustice but instead challenged unjust systems, whether it was his society's unjust treatment of lepers (Matt. 8:3; Mark 1:40-45; Luke 17:11-19) or the highly usurious money-lending system at the temple (Mark 11:15-19; 13:1-8).

The difficulty in maintaining a prophetic response is to remain aware of the ever-present and widespread denial of the ways in which social domination "confers entitlement, power, and status, and identifies certain people as undeserving of equal treatment."[25] As Christians we often think we are answering God's call to live in just and compassionate relationships within communities and across communities without realizing how we miss pieces of the picture and end up participating in oppressive relations, practices, and ideologies. To promote liberating thought and practice that would ensure a home for all in God's just and compassionate community requires, as West claims, both courage *and* vigilance.

Discussion Questions

1. What is your assessment of the responses to homelessness presented so far? Do the theological and philosophical emphases of AGRM and/or Habitat coincide with beliefs and practices in your faith community's responses to homelessness and poverty?

2. How can we recognize both the victimization and agency of the homeless and poor, and how do we avoid adopting perspectives that serve to oppress and label the people we think we are helping? Do you have examples of congregations or coalitions of congregations that have had some success being in solidarity with the homeless and poor?

3. How can faith communities make an effort to get to know people who are homeless? How do we avoid categorizing the homeless into the deserving and undeserving poor? Has your congregation changed aspects of its worship and community life to welcome the homeless?

4. How are both disruption and advocacy important in addressing homelessness and housing? What are some ways that faith communities can disrupt barriers to flourishing lives, and advocate for worldviews and policies that seek to make a home for everyone in God's just and compassionate community?

5. How do those faith communities and organizations that have ending homelessness and poverty as part of their mission not get caught up in ensuring the survival of their own institutional efforts? What resources and practices help faith communities to adopt and then maintain a prophetic response?

A Home for All in God's Just and Compassionate Community

Does advocating a prophetic-disruption approach mean that we remain in a constant mode of criticism? To promote justice and peace, we will continually have to resist injustices and violence. If our goal is to have just and compassionate communities where all people can flourish, then constructive organizing and advocacy for particular policies also will be necessary. While there might be differences in opinion as to how to address poverty and homelessness, groups from widely different theological perspectives and denominations *can* be united in the belief that Christian communities ought to be concerned about homelessness.

The challenge is how to move Christian communities to see and address the root causes of poverty and homelessness, in addition to ministering to those in need of direct hospitality and charity. There is no one perfect response to poverty and homelessness, but any adequate response must include both compassion and justice. It is vitally important that we disrupt the causes of poverty and homelessness and advocate for alternative visions and policies that promote flourishing lives for all. Neither disruption nor advocacy will help individuals or communities to flourish, however, if we do not have a deep level of compassion for *all* of our neighbors. Church communities can and should offer a strong moral voice and commitment to the movement for a just and compassionate world, but just as important, individual Christians and Christian communities must *practice* hospitality, compassion, and justice.

While many churches preach the values of hospitality, compassion, and justice, these are empty generalities apart from actual practices that consistently embody these values. Out of fear, most churches stop short of fulfilling these values. The fears get articulated in different ways, from liability concerns in letting homeless people sleep on church grounds to issues of safety and security for church members. Homeless activist and pastor Bill Kirlin-Hackett argues that safety and security are needs both the homeless and housed have in common. Our real problem, he argues, is our inability to see everyone as a neighbor.[1] Out of fear we try to protect ourselves and justify such protection by constructing stereotypes that turn our neighbors into "others" who are dangerous.

Church members might venture out and volunteer at a soup kitchen, shelter, or home build, and they might help struggling members within their congregation, but how many churches have opened their sanctuary doors to people who are homeless? How many churches have managed to avoid labeling particular groups of people and truly become hospitable and open communities that actively recruit neighbors who are "different"? Simply having an open-door policy does not mean that all people will feel welcome or at home. To become welcoming we must step outside of our "safe spaces" and become friends and neighbors with people on the margins. Of course, this is easier said than done in communities that are segregated by class and race barriers and in a competitive consumer economy that influences us to work long hours in order to chase the dream of material wealth. However, disruption of and resistance to such influences begins in our own lives and communities.

While practicing hospitality, compassion, and justice in our own lives and within our congregations is a first step, we also must ask what it means to take seriously our call to be disciples of Jesus Christ in our work in the world. Theologians Rita Nakashima Brock and Rebecca Parker describe the "ethical grace"[2] of Jesus as "love and generosity in community; care for all who have need, healing of the sick, appreciation for life, confrontation with powers of injustice and exploitation, and advocacy for freedom of the imprisoned."[3] Minister to the homeless Craig Rennebohm states the challenge of Christian mission this way:

I believe that we are called to offer more than individual first aid. We are called to share in work that shapes healing neighborhoods. When there is no inn, we are called to create places and programs of welcome and care. When our systems and institutions and policies and programs as a society fall short of supporting health and well-being, we are called to work together to make our community more just and humane, in concrete ways.[4]

Rennebohm argues that "we care for the soul of the world by caring for the souls of our neighbors, for each life that touches ours."[5] Compassionate responses of hospitality and charity, resistance to injustice and exploitation, and advocacy for systems and institutions that support justice and well-being are all equally important. The way of Jesus suggests a bottom-up approach that moves upward from caring for each person in our life to making a flourishing home for all in God's community.

Thus, hospitality must be connected to justice.[6] Hospitality as justice was a foundation of all morality in biblical times. Having been freed by God from slavery, the people of Israel understood that a covenant with God included caring for all within their midst by sharing their bread with the hungry and bringing the homeless poor into their houses (Isa. 58:7). Jesus also modeled hospitality as justice. At the Last Supper, and throughout his ministry, Jesus opened the banquet for all to be seated at the table in relationship with God and one another. Jesus envisioned abundant life for all, where humans are not only physically housed but are also truly at home within caring, inclusive, and sustainable communities. Paul sought to make such a vision of *koinonia* community a reality in the early church. Translations for *koinonia* include "fellowship," "contribution," "sharing," and "participation." The early church aimed to embody these values by caring for all its members, distributing goods according to need, and worshiping and praying together (Acts 2:42-47). Each member of the community participated fully in the fellowship and worship of the community because hospitality as justice was practiced with God's gifts shared sustainably by all.

The problem of homelessness is not simply about people who find themselves without a place to sleep. The problem of homelessness is a reflection of our collective identity as a people and a society. Our high value in the United States on individualism and each person's being responsible for him- or herself can hinder our ability to envision alternatives to what seems inevitable. Many Americans have been socialized to accept a dominant cultural worldview that promotes individual initiative, enterprise, and achieving the American Dream, but a society founded on such a competitive worldview privileges the winners and marginalizes the losers. The early church did not assume there must be losers, nor did they believe homelessness to be inevitable.

Jesus challenged those who tried to limit the seats at the banquet table and offer crumbs rather than abundant loaves. Hospitality as charity does not afford the recipients full human dignity in ways that enable them to participate fully in community and fellowship. The bountiful goods at the banquet table are not earned but are gifts from God, meant to be sustainably shared by all (including nonhuman creatures), not hoarded (Lev. 25:18-19, 23-24). All of God's creation is interdependent, with each living thing an intricate part contributing to the whole. Love of neighbor entails both being a neighbor to others and allowing others to be a neighbor to us. As the story of the starving widow who serves Elijah (1 Kings 17–18) attests, those who are poor and outcast can be just as hospitable as those who are rich and powerful.

While there is no single blueprint, there are basic levels of human and environmental flourishing for which we might aim. For one, all people in a society ought to have decent housing, access to adequate health care and a good education, and, if they are able, work that allows them to live healthy lives and contribute to a healthy society. For people who are not able to contribute through work, we ought to find other ways that they can contribute to society and have services and safety nets so they can live well. Basic goods are not all that is necessary for people to flourish, however. Meaningful avenues for participation for all individuals in communities and the broader society are also important. If we are all to participate in society and relate to one another as neighbors, there also needs to be a rearrangement of wealth and power. Substantial inequality as we have in our society today blocks solidarity between people and thwarts just and compassionate communities.

Charitable paternalism that sustains the status quo supplants solidarity and justice.

Sustainability requires that we think not only about how all are going to be seated at the table but also about how we are even going to have a table! Hospitality as justice entails that some of us must live more simply so that the earth can continue to sustain itself and its inhabitants. We must ask what type of houses and communities we are building. Sustainable hospitality requires structural changes that would move the housing industry's emphasis away from investment in high-end housing and toward earth-friendly housing and community planning. This would include increased commitment to mixed-income communities so that people who work in a community can more easily find affordable housing near their workplace, leaving more time for family and community life and lessening our society's dependence on fossil fuels. Such changes would promote the abundant life that Jesus envisioned.

Building a Social Movement to End Homelessness

All of our ideals of a just and compassionate society will be just that unless we have the political will and power to institute social change. Churches should not sit on the sidelines and claim that spiritual health is separate from physical and mental health, with the church responsible only for the former. The Hebrew prophets and Jesus emphasized both physical and spiritual well-being simultaneously. Promoting God's just and compassionate community has been the mission of many in the Christian tradition, and addressing issues of poverty has never been simply a liberal agenda. Many of today's conservative and evangelical Christians also are concerned about ending poverty and homelessness.

While it is not clear that either the Hebrew prophets or Jesus was trying to build a social movement per se, they were persistently reminding us of our responsibility to care for people on the margins, not simply with charity but by challenging unjust structural arrangements. Jesus exhorted his disciples to exhibit both compassion and justice. As the poem from Spanish poet Antonio Machado reminds us, Jesus wants us to wake up:

I love Jesus, who said to us:
Heaven and earth will pass away.
When heaven and earth have passed away,
my word will remain.
What was your word, Jesus?
Love? Affection? Forgiveness?
All your words were
one word: Wakeup![7]

Will we wake up to our responsibility to further God's "kin-dom" here on earth? Taking on this responsibility is not a ticket to salvation but is instead a response to the grace, love, and compassion God has shown us. Being part of a social movement promoting communities of compassion and justice flows from our created nature as relational beings made in God's image.

Why argue for a social movement? Have social movements not come and gone in the past? Can homelessness be addressed without creating a movement for social change? Some of the first recognized social movements were composed of working-class citizens organizing for better working conditions in the era of industrialization.[8] Social scientist Charles Tilly argues that social movements developed in the West after 1750 and included three elements: (1) a sustained organized public effort to make targeted claims on authorities; (2) use of political-action strategies, such as public meetings, rallies, petition drives, and creation of special-purpose coalitions; and (3) public representation that demonstrates moral worthiness, unity, numbers, and commitment of the constituency.[9] A social movement is not simply a one-time campaign but, rather, "a struggle engaging many parties, with each campaign centering on the repeated efforts of a shifting coalition to achieve a relatively well-defined set of political changes."[10]

A social movement against poverty and in support of redistribution of wealth and power is necessary if we are going to be successful at preventing homelessness and ensuring decent affordable housing for all. Such a grand agenda, however, would be an overwhelming place for most church congregations and individual Christians to start. Instead, they might adopt the way of Jesus, that is, a bottom-up approach that moves from care and compassion for each person to working with groups of people committed to making flourishing homes for all. While congregations are right to respond hospitably to direct need (compassion), they also need to be vocal and active in preventing poverty and homelessness (hospitality as justice).

Getting church members to wake up and embrace the vision of a social movement for just and compassionate communities takes education. Volunteering with charitable efforts to feed and shelter the homeless or build affordable housing can be a starting place if there is some critical reflection that accompanies the service. If people see the inadequacy of simply providing charity, they can begin to ask more critical questions about homelessness, thus opening the way for advocacy. Having a deeper understanding of the causes of homelessness will help to dispel the myths about who is homeless, opening the way for actual solidarity and compassion, which promotes justice.

Advocating for more affordable rental housing (not simply homeownership) should be at the top of the list for congregations wanting to do something about homelessness. While each community might address provision of low-income housing differently, relying solely on the efforts of nonprofits and churches to build and manage affordable rental housing will not suffice. Government intervention is necessary. While there needs to be more federal, state, and local funding allocated for creation of low-income rental housing and for low-income housing assistance, for those who are wary of "big government," there are other ways governments can be involved besides offering direct assistance. Local governments can create opportunities for affordable housing by zoning an adequate number of properties to allow for the development of rental housing, by adopting zoning laws that require developers to include a certain percentage of low-income rental housing in their developments, and by holding landlords accountable to fair rental practices and safety standards.

The federal government's program of Section 8 vouchers[11] is the only large-scale form of rental assistance available today, yet many recipients of these vouchers are unable to find landlords who will take vouchers, or they are unable to find safe and sanitary housing that fits their budget. (Voucher assistance is capped at a "fair market rent.")

Churches can be in solidarity with the homeless and working poor by advocating that both local and federal governments ensure the number of decent low-income rental housing units meets the need and that low-income renters are actually housed. While churches should support the availability of shelters so people do not have to sleep on the streets, there will be no end to the number of shelters needed if we do not address the lack of affordable housing.

In addition to public policy, we need to demand social responsibility on the part of the private sector. For example, as a condition of taxpayer money backing government insurance on bank deposits (not to mention federal bailouts), we can demand that banks provide low-interest loans for homebuyers. As a condition of receiving local zoning changes and building permits, we can demand that developers include low-income rental housing in their building plans. We have even more leverage if corporate entities receive tax subsidies. Some communities have required corporations who receive public assistance to provide a certain number of jobs, hire locally, pay a living wage, and offer health benefits. Other communities have required developers who receive public assistance to provide parking and build parks for local residents affected by new developments.[12] Currently, corporations play states, counties, and cities against one another to receive lucrative deals. Through public policy, we can eliminate such bidding, allowing communities instead to invest funds in community development.

A larger social movement will not only be concerned about policies related to poverty and housing, but it will also take on the even deeper issue of inequality of wealth and power. Adequately addressing inequality means critically analyzing our tax and budget structure and our political system. Without a change in our tax and budget system, we can advocate all we want to get more funds put toward ending homelessness, but we will be told there is no money. Thus, we must critically assess the ways that tax dollars go disproportionately toward better-off individuals and large corporations rather than the poor or even the middle class. Even more important to address is the amount of our federal budget that goes toward national defense. There never will be enough money for domestic economic and social programs unless we lower our military spending.[13]

Long-term solutions to eliminate poverty and homelessness will require changes in federal policy, as many decisions affecting poor, working-class, and middle-class Americans occur beyond cities, counties, and states. Changes in national policy will be made only if public opinion can be mobilized to support policies against poverty and oppression. Diversion of funds away from corporate subsidies and military expenditures would help not only the poor but also working- and middle-class families. Such funds could address basic health care for all, improved public schools and college aid, some form of universal child care, greater public transit, and access to affordable rental housing. Although housing assistance is only one of the areas just listed, all of these changes together would drastically lower the rate of homelessness.

In a social movement, there must be an organizational base that has an ability to mobilize. Groups must have the power to affect change: to promote policies, to hold government and corporate leaders accountable, and to create programs. Ideally, an organizational base of people for justice can work with government and corporate leaders to address societal issues. Such cooperative endeavors happen. Realistically, if the change sought is a redistribution of wealth and power and an end to violence and oppression, there will be conflict with and resistance from those in power. Thus, Christian ethicist Reinhold Niebuhr has argued, "Since it is impossible to count on enough moral goodwill among those who possess irresponsible power to sacrifice it for the good of the whole, it must be destroyed by coercive methods and these will always run the peril of introducing new forms of injustice in place of those abolished."[14] Coercive methods can feel un-Christian to many church people, but resistance and advocacy for social change can be peaceful and nonviolent. Moreover, justice clearly requires both resistance and advocacy, as Moses, the Hebrew prophets, Jesus, and others demonstrate in scriptural stories. Martin Luther King Jr. gave us excellent advice when he said, "We must combine the toughness of the serpent and the softness of the dove, a tough mind and a tender heart." That is, we should oppose the unjust system while at the same time loving the perpetrators of the system (which are ourselves).[15]

While eliminating poverty, homelessness, and oppression are vital end goals, the process of social change is also important, especially since there always will be the temptation to substitute new forms of injustice. A social movement will be successful if it has developed the leadership potential of people committed over the long haul to promote flourishing communities, even if particular campaigns for change fail. Such leaders will be of a tough mind and a tender heart, exhibiting compassion while simultaneously disrupting injustice.

Congregational Listening, Educating, Advocating, and Organizing

Ending poverty and homelessness is a goal shared by Christians from different theological backgrounds and denominations. Many congregations are doing more than paying lip service to the goal. Some congregations have worked to find ways to make their communities open and welcoming to people of all stations in life. Others have organized to respond to the needs of people who are marginalized in their local communities and cities through creation of programs and through advocacy for particular city and county policies. Still others are proactively advocating for antipoverty policies at state and national levels. An approach of prophetic disruption will include all of these forms.

One of the problems homeless advocates have encountered in working with churches on the issue of homelessness is what Bill Kirlin-Hackett refers to as "siloing," where each church is a separate silo and churches are not working together to address homelessness.[16] Paul Christie, the former executive director of Hands on Hartford in Connecticut, says that while churches claim to value cooperative work, they also are drawn to creating their own program(s) that they run exclusively and that develop relationships among members.[17] The result is a patchwork of services, with some services overlapping while other needs go unmet, as well as competition for scarce resources. The premise of a social movement is that we work together in promoting just and compassionate communities. The goal is not to protect our own kingdoms but to further the kin-dom of God. This means, for example, reaching beyond simply meeting with other churches of the same denomination. It entails working with secular organizations, other religious traditions, and even other Christian churches with a different theological world-view. Such networking can be difficult for small churches struggling simply to survive, but there are ecumenical organizations that help to bring churches together in organizational efforts.

Many organizing efforts use common strategic approaches but do not form a movement because there is no coordination among groups. The result is often modest local achievements, and very little influence on the national agenda or even state agendas. In past social movements, such as the labor union movement in the early 1900s and the civil rights movement of the 1960s, there were separate campaigns and constit-uencies, but there was a common purpose that gave momentum for larger policy change at the national level. Without a movement to influ-ence federal policy, there is a limited amount that groups can achieve at the local level because cities and states are facing such heavy bud-get deficits. Holding corporations accountable also takes a coordinated approach, as most corporate branch managers do not have a stake in local communities, and decision-making occurs at corporate headquar-ters far from the community.[18]

Another problem is that churches often respond to social problems in ways that reflect their own values and biases rather than listening to the needs and desires of the people who are experiencing a social injus-tice like homelessness. For example, a group of homeless people formed a tent city in Seattle, complete with their own governmental structure. Churches wanted to help out, but instead of listening to what the home-less said their need was (e.g., land), they bought them a shower and served them meals. The shower still sits on the truck unused, while the camp members continue to struggle with the city government over where they may set up their tents.[19] Since Seattle officials have ruled that the tent city can be set up only for a limited time in any one area, a shower is seen by tent-city residents as extra baggage when it comes time to move. Many church members approach homelessness as prob-lem solvers instead of listeners. With this mentality, most encounters with the homeless are "transactions" (e.g., offering food, motel vouch-ers, services), and no deeper relationship of trust is developed.

Another premise of social movements is solidarity with those who are marginalized and exploited. The residents of the Seattle tent city have elected their own leaders, and these leaders have clearly stated the needs of the community, sometimes even saying no to ideas church members propose. While a tent city might not be what church people had in mind, nor is it necessarily the long-term solution to inadequate housing, it is meeting a current need and is being organized by the homeless themselves. Thus, churches ought to work with these tent-city leaders in addressing their immediate needs while also advocating together for more long-term solutions. Solidarity will occur when church members develop relationships with the homeless, listen to what their actual needs are, and support in ways that empower not patronize.

The issue of listening to the homeless is complex. The people most readily identified as homeless are the chronically homeless we see on the streets. Their needs are likely to be different than those of people who are working and only episodically homeless. While both the working-class and the jobless poor want the opportunity to live flourishing lives, their interests are not always the same in particular cases. Identifying the different interests at play in any one situation is strategically important so that the powers that be do not use groups against one another to thwart deep-seated change.[20] Working with larger ecumenical and interfaith groups that have professional organizers can help churches to avoid participating in nonprophetic actions. While all people should be able to participate and be heard in society, not everyone's perspective supports prophetic change. Listening to subjugated voices is crucial to understanding homelessness and poverty and to holding accountable the powers that be, yet we still must sort through the voices to determine what actions and policy will be most likely to support justice and compassion.

Listen to Homeless in Community

Finding ways for church members to get to know personally people who are homeless or marginalized is often what promotes changes in a church's mission and participation in advocacy efforts. Some churches have become radically inclusive by orienting their mission toward supporting the homeless and by developing outreach and worship that appeals to people in all walks of life. Glide Memorial United Methodist Church in San Francisco, for example, has been "building a church without walls" by welcoming everyone, offering unconditional love, and valuing differences. Attending a Glide church service is a joyous event with lots of singing, dancing, and celebration. Even more noticeable, however, is the diversity of people in attendance. In the choir, a homeless person might be singing next to a well-known San Francisco personality, and congregants are all shades of color.[21]

Glide provides a range of services for the homeless and poor, including a shelter, drop-in center, soup kitchen, medical clinic, low-income housing, youth programs, and women's center. But even more importantly, the homeless and poor are members of the worshiping community. While Glide Memorial Church emphasizes recovery and personal transformation (with the stance that we are all in recovery), it seeks also to change the world. Its embodiment of radical inclusion and compassion has led to its continual involvement in advocacy against poverty, homelessness, unjust wars, and oppression.[22]

Churches can find ways for parishioners to listen to the homeless without taking on the management of a shelter or soup kitchen. Saint Leo's Church in Tacoma, Washington, created two programs to connect parishioners with the homeless in their area. In this church's "Walkabouters and Talkabouters" program, parishioners walk around the neighborhood and get acquainted with people eating at the Hospitality Kitchen. In their "Sandwich Brigade" program, parishioners make and distribute sandwiches to the homeless.[23] Emanuel Lutheran Church in Hartford, Connecticut, sponsored a Servant Day where one hundred members of its congregation divided up into community-service teams to address issues of poverty and homelessness in its city. The participants gathered afterward for worship and for reflection that led to a social justice emphasis in worship and further service projects.[24]

The National Coalition for the Homelessness (NCH) offers a manual for groups wishing to set up homelessness speakers' bureaus.[25] Homeless and formerly homeless people are given training to be able to tell their stories to different groups. Up to three people with diverse stories and backgrounds will speak to any one group. NCH suggests showing a short video to assist in the educational effort and having the presenters share their story for ten minutes, leaving plenty of time for questions and discussion. My experience of homelessness speakers' bureaus is that personal stories of why people became homeless are more effective at dispelling myths about homelessness than any recitation of statistics.

In several areas, churches have supported and been involved with the burgeoning number of tent cities that have sprung up since the mortgage foreclosure crisis and resulting recession. Many tent cities have been organized by the homeless themselves, with rules of zero tolerance for violence, sexual harassment, drug or alcohol use, or prostitution. The tent cities serve not only as a place of shelter but also as a political statement on the lack of affordable housing. Coalitions of churches have supported these cities with donations and places to camp and have stood in solidarity with the homeless in advocating for adequate and affordable housing. Through their involvement, church members are able to see the homeless organizing themselves and articulating their own needs, challenging the stereotypes of them as homeless victims in need of rescue. Church members also become aware, however, that the homeless do need those with power and privilege to advocate with them for such things as affordable housing, jobs with living wages, and access to health care.

These church members and church communities have realized that understanding homelessness and having compassion for people who experience homelessness entails getting to know people who are homeless. They take seriously the claim that we must start by listening to people who experience the problems we are trying to address. Congregations might start through service but hopefully will take the next step of making their worship service and church programs inclusive of all class levels, including the chronically homeless. Critical reflection and educational efforts can help congregants avoid treating people as "other." Bonds of solidarity can be formed and community life can be enriched in congregations with an orientation of radical inclusivity.

Educate Parishioners and Community Leaders

Since education is often the first step in getting church members to participate in a social movement, efforts within congregations to incorporate the mission of promoting a just and compassionate society into their worship practices, their educational efforts, and their community interactions are crucial. Many of the previous examples of church engagement included an educational component. The following are two organizations that have oriented their educational efforts nationally.

Luther Place Memorial Church in Washington, D.C., made a decision to reorient its mission radically. In the 1970s, when homelessness was an increasing phenomenon, Luther Place opened its church building to shelter the homeless. The church now has many services addressing homelessness: a drop-in center, a night shelter, group homes for women living with mental illness, single-room-occupancy apartments, a wellness center, and affordable rental housing for low-income families. Its decision to become a congregation of hospitality changed many aspects of its worship, outreach, and membership and prompted it to offer more far-reaching educational programs.

In particular, Luther Place created two distinctive programs to influence and educate Christians to participate in a social movement for justice and compassion: the Steinbruck Center for Urban Studies and Lutheran Volunteer Corps. The Steinbruck Center offers intensive programs for church youth groups, congregations, and college students that educate participants about homelessness and poverty, assist them to see the connections between faith and justice, and prompt them to envision ways to be part of the movement for justice and compassion.[26] Groups generally come to the center for anywhere from two to seven days and are involved in a number of educational endeavors, which include such activities as participating in a homelessness simulation game, listening to stories of people who are homeless, studying the Bible in light of homelessness, visiting advocacy groups, staying in a shelter overnight, working in a food pantry, and touring the city.

Originally started by Luther Place Church, Lutheran Volunteer Corps is now a Lutheran nonprofit organization and has volunteer communities and placements in cities across the nation.[27] In Lutheran Volunteer Corps, adults over twenty-one (commonly postcollege) commit to working for justice and living in intentional household communities that aim to promote deepened spirituality and simple, sustainable living. This program takes seriously the notion that being part of a social movement means living within community and requires intentional commitment.

Another institution in Washington, D.C., with national educational outreach is Sojourners, a progressive evangelical organization. Its aim is to influence communities of faith to adopt a social justice perspective, with the goal of creating a social movement and influencing public policies. Sojourners is especially good at educating and mobilizing a large number of people through media, both print and electronic. Its magazine, *Sojourners,* is most widely known, but in addition it has an online newsletter, blog, and Web site. Further, in 2006 it created a network of churches that get weekly social justice resource materials for sermons, worship, and educational purposes.[28]

While Sojourners works with congregations across the theological and political spectrum, historically it has been connected to evangelical churches. Its work has served to challenge the understanding of "moral values" in evangelical circles to include particular attention to the issues of war, human rights, environmental injustice, and poverty. Sojourners now has a network of nine hundred "faith and justice" churches that address these issues.[29] A key focus in 2009 was a "mobilization to end poverty." Sojourners argues that overcoming poverty requires vision and commitment, and its goal is for our society to reduce the number of Americans living in poverty by half in the next ten years. It also supports the Millennium Development Goals, agreed to by 189 world leaders, to address extreme global poverty.[30]

Many congregations will start by getting their parishioners involved in direct service and from there broaden parishioner understandings of discipleship to include justice as well as charity. Too often, social justice work gets relegated to a committee and is not incorporated into the whole mission and life of the church. The more parishioners a congregation has involved with the poor and homeless, the more likely it will be to embrace a movement to end poverty and homelessness. Being confronted with the realities that people in poverty face and hearing their stories makes poverty and homelessness real to people, hopefully motivating them to confront the societal causes.

Join Local Coalitions Working to End Homelessness

To be more effective in ending homelessness, individual congregations can join coalitions of churches working together. Such coalitions exist in most major cities. Some of the coalitions are organized to offer direct services only; others combine direct service and advocacy to prevent and end homelessness; and still others only focus on advocacy. Congregations also can be involved in existing programs that address hunger and homelessness.

Most prevalent are the coalitions that offer direct services. Silver Spring Interfaith Housing Coalition, near Washington, D.C., is composed of around twenty-five congregations. It has low-income housing units for people, mentoring programs, and support for women re-entering the community from prison.[31] Churches United for the Homeless in Moorhead, Minnesota, with fifty-eight member churches, offers shelter, food, and case management.[32] Hands on Hartford in Hartford, Connecticut, with twelve member churches, works with congregations on community engagement and provides housing, food, fuel, and support services for children and families.[33] These coalitions do some advocacy in their local regions, but most of their efforts are focused on addressing direct need.

In many urban areas, communities have employed gardening as a means of addressing both hunger and homelessness. Some programs intentionally employ the homeless in a community garden, while others work with low-income individuals who might be, but are not necessarily, homeless. Started by college student David Baron, HOPE Gardens in Chapel Hill, North Carolina, accepts applications from individuals living on the streets or in shelters.[34] Rent from leasing plots to community members pays for supplies and wages for the homeless participants. Coming to the garden gives the homeless a place to go during the day, and the process of planting, cultivating, and harvesting the crops, then selling them at farmers' markets, brings a sense of accomplishment.[35] Churches could be involved in existing projects like this or could work with a coalition of churches to start their own.

Della Spearman sees her work with community gardening as part of her Christian ministry. Della works through the Sullivan Center in Atlanta. Founded by Sister Marie, this organization helps people remain self-sufficient.[36] The goal of Della's organic garden project is to end poverty and hunger through education. She especially works to educate youth about gardening and healthy food. In addition, she sells the produce at farmers' markets with attention to making sure Women, Infant and Children (WIC) food vouchers are accepted as payment. She also donates food that is left over to area food pantries (over three hundred pounds since its inception two years ago). Della's focus is to address homelessness and poverty while preserving the dignity of people. She realizes that many people do not like to be classified as homeless due to the stigma attached, so she opens her gardening project to any low-income participants no matter what their housing status.[37]

Other church coalitions have emphasized education and advocacy. The Interfaith Task Force on Homelessness in Seattle developed as a vehicle for the religious community to exhort leaders in the public, business, nonprofit, and private sectors to end homelessness and create affordable supportive housing.[38] Formed from a conference attended by 350 religious and community representatives, the task force aims to create a political will to end homelessness. The task force's main strategy is to get a broad range of churches to work together on practical actions to support the homeless. Out of these efforts, more long-term advocacy for particular policies, such as affordable rental housing, has emerged. To get churches engaged, it educates congregations on homelessness through a curriculum series, guest preaching and speaking engagements, and an annual conference. It also educates elected officials and has a seat on many of the boards addressing the issues of homelessness and affordable housing. While the task force focuses narrowly on homelessness and housing, it supports other antipoverty advocacy efforts as well.

The Metro Interfaith Coalition for Affordable Housing (MICAH) in Minneapolis/St. Paul was developed to wage local and regional policy campaigns for shifting public resources to affordable housing.[39] MICAH is organized into six chapters connected to regional areas in the Twin Cities. Each chapter has regular meetings and roundtable discussions to mobilize support and community engagement on specific local and citywide policy initiatives on affordable housing, zoning, and land use. MICAH also does a considerable amount of educational work with congregations and community leaders.

Local coalitions of churches can solve the problem of churches "siloing" and can offer a stronger moral voice on social issues such as homelessness. When churches work together, they have more power to hold government officials and business leaders accountable and to promote city and county policies that benefit the poor and marginalized. While national policies might be needed to address some issues, much can be accomplished at the local level. For example, coalitions of churches, along with other grassroots organizations, can advocate for the elimination of laws that criminalize the homeless, such as anti-camping, loitering, or panhandling ordinances. They can push for an adequate number of shelters and transitional housing units to serve the homeless. They can encourage policies that support affordable rental housing, especially inclusionary zoning ordinances that require a percentage of affordable rental units in all new housing developments. Finally, they can advocate for laws, or enforcement of already existing laws, that protect renters from discrimination.

Organize Churches to Advocate for State and National Policies

There are several national ecumenical and interfaith organizations that work locally with coalitions of churches and mobilize groups to advocate for state and national policies. While they do not all address homelessness and housing directly, their emphases on issues of poverty and worker justice support the goal of ending homelessness. I will look at two such examples, PICO National Network (originally Pacific Institute for Community Organizations) and the Industrial Areas Foundation (IAF). While both are national organizations, the affiliates of each are concentrated in different regional areas. They have similar philosophies, as PICO developed out of the IAF organizing model. Their distinctive emphasis on organizing people from the ground up is a useful approach for responding to the issues that most affect the poor and homeless. In this section, I will explain PICO's organizing philosophy and highlight some of the work both PICO and IAF are doing. In the next section, I will share another of IAF's projects.

Started by a Catholic priest, PICO has grown to fifty-three affiliated interfaith federations working in one hundred cities and towns and seventeen states.[40] PICO organizes on a range of issues, from school improvement to accessible health care to affordable housing.[41] Started by Saul Alinsky in the 1940s, IAF has grown to fifty-nine local organizations in twenty-one states, Canada, the United Kingdom, and Germany.[42] Currently, IAF is focusing on the living-wage movement, affordable owner-occupied homes, and large-scale blight removal.[43]

By having a number of faith-based organizing federations, PICO allows church congregations to support their ethical convictions in the public realm. PICO staff works directly with coalitions of congregations to identify and address local areas of concern. PICO works mainly in low-income communities so that people who are more likely to be marginalized can have a say in the decisions that shape their lives. PICO staff offers leadership training and works directly with the congregations to help them negotiate with and hold accountable public officials. Sociologist Richard Wood calls the PICO model "structural symbiosis," whereby churches can be involved with reform in the social world without taking on the political demands of organizing.[44] For PICO, the ability to mobilize is central to gaining the power to effect change in a democratic society, thus its approach is centered on organizing. While it acknowledges government can play a role in a better society, PICO believes civic leaders and organizations must have power to influence policy.[45]

PICO contrasts its organizing approach to a service, education, self-help, or advocacy approach. On its Web site, it offers the following example of the differences:

> Suppose an organizer encountered a situation in which there were a large number of homeless people in the community.
> - If the organizer went out and started convincing neighborhood religious institutions to put cots in their basements for the homeless, that would be a *service* approach. The organizer, and the congregations would be doing a direct service for people.
> - If the organizer started doing studies about the causes of homelessness and how it was dealt with in other cities, and then distributed the information, that is an *education* approach. There are many groups that exist mainly to educate people about some social issue.
> - If the organizer began to hold workshops for homeless people about how to find a house or a job, that would be a *self-help*

approach. The idea is that people can solve their problem by improving themselves or their knowledge of themselves, and that they can often do it better in groups.

- If the organizer went down to City Hall to lobby to get the city to open shelters and food programs, that would be an *advocacy* approach. The people without homes would not necessarily be involved or even know that the organizer was doing it.

- If the organizer started talking to homeless people and organized a large number of them to first decide on the solutions that they wanted, and then to pressure the city to win those solutions, that would be an *organizing* approach. The people directly affected by the problem, whatever it is, take action to win a solution.[46]

PICO federations have had the most success influencing policy on local issues by focusing on the relationships among participants rather than supporting any one ideological position. Organizers focus on religious motivations and teachings rather than political affiliations. While PICO advocates systematic change at all levels of government, it starts with local issues before moving upward to address issues at a city, state, or national level. This process gives it a deeply rooted foundation in local communities that promotes participation and successful mobilization.[47] Increasingly, however, PICO has realized the need for organizing at the national level and has moved to broaden its work in that direction.

Affordable housing has been a local issue of concern in many communities, and PICO has had good success in organizing on the issue. Local federations have won "new mixed-income housing development, comprehensive neighborhood reinvestment strategies, inclusionary-zoning ordinances, renter protections, housing trust funds and first time homeownership programs."[48] For example, L.A. Voice, a PICO federation, has been involved with a coalition of housing organizations to get a majority of city council members to sign on to a platform for new city policies on housing. On the national level, a PICO group calling itself the "Recovery Express" (consisting of families at risk of foreclosure or having already lost their homes) did an eight-city tour en route to Washington, D.C., to urge Congress and banks to support plans announced by the federal government to help families stay in their homes. In each city, prayer vigils and rallies were held to mobilize support for the issue.[49]

IAF has organized to clean up blighted areas without displacing residents. With multiple congregations in East Brooklyn, they started building homes in run-down areas, supporting homeownership for low-income families through a community development corporation titled Nehemiah Corporation of America. They since have worked with other church coalitions in South Bronx, Baltimore, Philadelphia, and Washington, D.C. Building homes led to pressuring city councils to remove blight and reconstruct areas in ways that benefit low-income residents. This organizing led to the passage of a $295-million blight-removal bond issue in Philadelphia and a $100-million bond issue in Washington, D.C.[50]

The strength of this organizing approach is that it starts with issues that are central to particular communities, ensuring that congregations will be part of the process of empowerment. It also involves congregations in a prophetic approach by addressing structural injustices. While PICO and IAF focus on organizing, the end goal is always advocacy of particular policies and actions to improve communities. Some policies and actions are addressed at the local level, while others will be addressed at the state or national levels.

Stand in Solidarity with Workers

While not all of the homeless can work (often due to disabilities), a significant number can and want to. Many people in so-called unskilled labor positions have dealt with significant workplace injustices, from harassment to wage theft to unsafe working conditions. Industrial Areas Foundation (IAF) designed and organized for passage of the first living-wage bill in Baltimore, in 1994, leading to similar bills in over one hundred communities. Interfaith Worker Justice (IWJ), with a network of seventy interfaith committees, workers' centers, and student groups, seeks to strengthen the religious community's involvement in issues of workplace justice. IWJ does not focus on housing issues, but it helps to address some of the root causes of homelessness by organizing to improve wages, benefits, and working conditions for workers in low-wage jobs.[51]

Baltimoreans United in Leadership Development (BUILD), an affiliate of IAF, was the first community organization to negotiate successfully a city living-wage ordinance. In response to the part-time and low-wage jobs of Baltimore's massive Inner Harbor tourist development of new hotels, restaurants, and shops, as well as a stadium and convention center, BUILD organized workers into a negotiating organization called the Solidarity Sponsoring Committee. Madison Avenue Presbyterian Church's pastor was the president of BUILD at this time, and his church and others supported the workers in their organizing efforts. The resulting agreement with the Baltimore City Council set a higher city minimum wage, recognized the workers' negotiating organization, and required that all vendors who contract with the city must pay the new wage.[52]

IWJ's vision is one where "all workers share in the prosperity of our society, enjoy the fundamental human right to organize, and lead dignified lives as a result of their labor."[53] IWJ works toward its vision in several ways. It stands in solidarity with workers when they are organizing for better working conditions and remuneration, and it advocates for public policy that supports the rights of workers. It also educates by offering social and economic justice educational and organizing resources to congregations and by conducting worker justice summer internships for undergraduate and seminary students and alternative break immersions for college students. Congregations and individuals are involved with IWJ through local affiliate interfaith committees or worker centers that support laborers in specific geographical areas.

The biggest problem the worker centers are faced with is wage theft, that is, "people not getting paid for their work." Executive director Kim Bobo explains in her book *Wage Theft in America* the many ways that employers cheat workers out of pay, and she offers solutions to the problem. While there are laws in place to address wage theft, there is little enforcement of the laws, and workers do not have the time or information to file complaints. Thus, the laws fail to protect workers. IWJ supports unions as vital to society and the protection of workers, but Bobo argues that unions and worker centers alone are not enough. Of crucial importance to protecting workers is a strengthened U.S. Department of Labor that can adequately address worker justice.

While standing in solidarity with workers is not a strategy directly aimed at ending homelessness, it is equally as effective. The workers that organizations like IAF and IWJ help are financially on the margins. Low pay, stolen wages, or unjust job loss can mean the difference between having a roof over one's head and sleeping in a car. Prophetically responding to homelessness can be done by addressing a whole host of issues, from making health care accessible to promoting affordable and quality child care to improving low-performing public schools. The goal of a prophetic response is to prevent homelessness by changing policies and structures that cause poverty.

Conclusion

All of these examples of listening, educating, advocating, and organizing are attempts to be part of a social movement for justice and compassion. The congregations and individuals involved understand that we must change aspects of our society to address the roots of homelessness. If we examined any of these strategies in depth, we would find faults and realize that not all organizing and educational efforts achieve their goals. But what is more important is the process of acting in solidarity with people on the margins. Solidarity is no easy task in a society unequally structured around power differences based on class, race, gender, and other means of differentiating people, but if we take seriously Jesus' call to discipleship, solidarity is not an option but a responsibility. This chapter has laid out a number of ways in which churches and individual Christians can fulfill this responsibility. While there are many approaches, the most important thing is to take action.

Individual Christians, churches, and religious organizations involved in charitable approaches to the problem of homelessness have already begun to take action, but their responses are not enough. Charitable approaches can be compassionate but fall still short of justice. Since they do not challenge structural inequity of wealth, power, and privilege in our society, they fail to prevent the problems of home-lessness and substandard housing and often reinforce the oppressive notion that the homeless and poor alone are to blame for their plight. Addressing direct need and promoting homeownership for low-income families should continue, but ideally we will become a more just society that relies less on charity. Embracing a Christian approach of prophetic disruption entails working with others both to challenge oppression and inequality and to advocate and organize strategically for social and economic policies that create a home for all. In solidarity with the poor and homeless, we can create and participate in communities that foster physical and spiritual wholeness.

Discussion Questions

1. Has your faith community stopped short of fully practicing hospi-tality, compassion, and justice out of fear? How so?

2. Are homelessness and poverty simply inevitable aspects of modern industrial societies? If not, what is your vision of a just and compas-sionate society, and what must change in American society to reach this vision?

3. What does it mean to take seriously our call to be disciples of Jesus Christ in mission and exhibit "ethical grace"? What does it mean to open up our understanding of hospitality to include justice as well as compassion? What would have to change in our individual and congregational lives for us to embrace this vision?

4. Congregations from radically different theological perspectives can be part of a social movement to end homelessness and poverty, and there are multiple ways congregations can be involved. How can your congregation start from the bottom up and become part of a larger network of groups working toward a just and compas-sionate society?

5. How will you and your faith community "wake up" and work to end homelessness and poverty in our country? Will your efforts address distribution of wealth and power in our country, and will they develop the leadership potential of people for justice-making over the long haul?

Notes

Introduction

1. Jesse McKinley, "Cities Deal With a Surge in Shantytowns," *New York Times*, March 26, 2009, http://www.nytimes.com/2009/03/26/us/26tents.html, "As Jobs Vanish, Motel Rooms Become Home," *New York Times*, March 11, 2009, http://www.nytimes.com/2009/03/11/us/11motel.html; Katharine Q. Seelye, "Sacramento and Its Riverside Tent City," *New York Times*, March 11, 2009, http://thelede.blogs.nytimes.com/2009/03/11/tent-city-report/; all accessed October 27, 2010.

2. Alex Kotlowitz, "All Boarded Up," *New York Times Magazine*, March 8, 2009, http://www.nytimes.com/2009/03/08/magazine/08Foreclosure-t.html; Catherine Rampell, "Painting Lawns Green," *New York Times*, March 30, 2009, http://economix.blogs.nytimes.com/2009/03/30/painting-lawns-green/ (the city of Perris, California, hired a contractor to spray-paint brown lawns of abandoned homes); both accessed October 27, 2010.

3. Seelye, "Sacramento and Its Riverside Tent City.

4. See Jill Suzanne Shook, ed., *Making Housing Happen: Faith-based Affordable Housing Models* (St. Louis: Chalice), 2006.

5. I will draw primarily from Traci C. West's two books: *Wounds of the Spirit: Black Women, Violence, and Resistance Ethics* (New York: New York University Press, 1999), and *Disruptive Christian Ethics: When Racism and Women's Lives Matter* (Louisville: Westminster John Knox, 2006).

1. Solidarity with the Homeless

1. Traci C. West, *Disruptive Christian Ethics: When Racism and Women's Lives Matter* (Louisville: Westminster John Knox, 2006), xi–xii.

2. Traci C. West, *Wounds of the Spirit: Black Women, Violence, and Resistance Ethics* (New York: New York University Press, 1999), 4.

3. West, *Disruptive Christian Ethics*, 4.

4. Ibid., 69.
5. West, *Wounds of the Spirit*, 11–12.
6. West, *Disruptive Christian Ethics*, 48.
7. West, *Wounds of the Spirit*, 100–121.
8. Ibid., 155.
9. West, *Disruptive Christian Ethics*, 68.
10. Ibid., 54.
11. Ibid., 47.
12. Ibid., 56–57.
13. West, *Wounds of the Spirit*, 156.
14. Meredith L. Ralston, *"Nobody Wants to Hear Our Truth": Homeless Women and Theories of the Welfare State* (Westport, Conn.: Greenwood, 1996), 81–89.
15. West, *Wounds of the Spirit*, 151.
16. Ibid., 161.
17. Ibid., 153–58.
18. Ibid., 162.
19. Ibid., 187–88.
20. Many cities have homeless newspapers that share news stories related to the problem of homelessness and housing, offer a venue for homeless people to share their writing, and serve as a way for homeless people to earn money on the streets. There are also several Internet sites devoted to the work of homeless people. One such example is the Homeless Poets' Café, http://www.ipoet.com, accessed October 28, 2010.
21. Claire J. Baker, "Truce on War," *Street Spirit: Homeless News & Homeless Blues in the Bay Area*, December 2006, http://www.thestreetspirit.org/Dec2006/poems.htm, accessed October 28, 2010.
22. West, *Wounds of the Spirit*, 190.
23. Ibid., 199–207.
24. West, *Disruptive Christian Ethics*, 54.

2. Homelessness and Housing in the United States

1. Martha Burt, Laudan Y. Aron, Edgar Lee, and Jesse Valente, *Helping America's Homeless: Emergency Shelter or Affordable Housing?* (Washington, D.C.: The Urban Institute Press, 2001), 5.
2. For example: "Of 6834 [Presbyterian] congregations that responded to questions about their involvement in ministries in homelessness and housing in 2006, over 53 percent indicated that they had provided either volunteers or financial support or both to a ministry with persons who are homeless or in need of housing assistance. Responses show that both financial support and volunteers were nearly evenly split between Habitat for Humanity and other ministries." Question 15, Stated Clerk's Annual Questionnaire for Year Ending December 31, 2006, Presbyterian Church (U.S.A.). Quoted from Advisory Committee on Social Witness Policy, *From Home-*

lessness to Hope: Constructing Just, Sustainable Communities For All God's People (June 2008), 15, http://www.pcusa.org/resource/homelessness-hope-constructing-just-sustainable-co/, accessed October 29, 2010.

3. The lowest rate of homeownership was 44 percent in 1940, right after the Great Depression. U.S. Census Bureau, Census of Housing, http://www.census.gov/hhes/www/housing/census/historic/owner.html, accessed October 29, 2010.

4. Since 2004, the ownership rate has been dropping fast, to 67.8 percent in early 2008. Rachel L. Swarns, "Rise in Renters Erasing Gains for Ownership," *New York Times*, June 21, 2008. Even at the height of homeownership, blacks and Hispanics generally had a 20 percent lower homeownership rate than whites. In 2005, the homeownership rate for blacks was 48.8 percent, and for Hispanics was 49.5 percent. Source: HUD and U.S. Census Bureau, found in Lawrence L. Thompson, *A History of HUD*, 14, http://mysite.verizon.net/hudhistory/, accessed October 29, 2010.

5. The one exception has been the 1990s, when the economy by traditional standards was doing well. Other factors have influenced the rate of homelessness more recently, namely wage levels in comparison to the cost of housing, health care, other daily expenses, and the lack of affordable housing.

6. Kenneth L. Kusmer, *Down and Out, On the Road: The Homeless in American History* (New York: Oxford University Press, 2002), 36–38.

7. Todd Depastino, *Citizen Hobo: How a Century of Homelessness Shaped America* (Chicago: University of Chicago Press, 2003), 8.

8. Unemployment did not become a widespread phenomenon until industrialization. Ibid., 6–8.

9. Kusmer, *Down and Out, On the Road*, 26–58.

10. The presence of homeless women went against the prevailing "dependent womanhood" ideology. Women weren't "on the road" due to harassment, violence, and a lack of public services such as police lodging open to them. Charitable organizations offered institutions that housed them and put them to work. Depastino, *Citizen Hobo*, 13.

11. African Americans had not been in the "army of tramps" since southern white planters had kept workers in place through debt peonage, vagrancy ordinances, and low wages. Tramping was also dangerous for blacks due to racism. Ibid., 14.

12. Reformers also organized to have police-station facilities for the homeless closed down since such facilities encouraged drunkenness and indolence by housing the "unworthy."

13. These religious missions did not use work tests or inquire into the background of the men before serving them, as all were considered "worthy" of assistance. Kusmer, *Down and Out, On the Road*, 88–91.

14. Ibid., 162.

15. Men of color also received assistance, but often in segregated camps. Ibid., 216.

16. Ibid., 211–17.

17. "Urge Prison Camp Hard Labor for 'Box Car Tourists,'" *Los Angeles Herald-Express*,

February 4, 1936, http://newdeal.feri.org/tolan/tol09.htm#b, accessed October 29, 2010.

18. Kusmer, *Down and Out, On the Road*, 224.

19. Studies from 1958 and 1966 showed that from one-third to one-half of the skid-row men were employed. Five factors that influenced unemployment were: (1) seasonal occupations; (2) disability or sickness; (3) old age, and inability to compete with younger workers; (4) alcoholism; and (5) laziness. Focus is usually on the last two factors, but according to Howard Bahr they account for less than half of the unemployment on skid row. Howard M. Bahr, *Skid Row: An Introduction to Disaffiliation* (New York: Oxford University Press, 1973), 95–97.

20. Ibid., 87.

21. "The most common facility at the turn of the century was the cage hotel. These were lofts or other large, open buildings that were subdivided into tiny cubicles using boards or sheets of corrugated iron. Since these walls were always one to three feet short of the floor or ceiling, the open space was sealed off with chicken wire, hence the name 'cage hotels.' Heat, lighting, ventilation, and sanitary conditions were abysmal and owners could pack as many as 200 men on a floor. Estimates are that this form of housing provided shelter for as many as 40,000 to 60,000 people during the winter." Robert A. Slayton, "Single Room Occupancy Hotels, " in *Encyclopedia of Chicago*, ed. Janice L. Reiff, Ann Durkin Keating, and James R. Grossman. http://www.encyclopedia.chicagohistory.org/pages/613.html, accessed October 29, 2010.

22. In 1940, 50 percent of housing units lacked adequate plumbing and 20 percent were in need of major repairs. Most slum housing was poorly constructed to start with. Thompson, *A History of HUD*, 4.

23. Lawrence J. Vale, *From the Puritans to the Projects: Public Housing and Public Neighbors* (Cambridge, Mass.: Harvard University Press, 2000), 8.

24. Ibid., 15.

25. Thompson, *A History of HUD*, 4.

26. "In 1934, when Congress created the FHA, about half the residential mortgages in the country were in Depression-related default. It was difficult for young families to buy their own homes: residential mortgages were interest-only instruments with the principal falling due after only five to ten years. The typical down payment was 50 percent of the purchase price. The FHA invented the long-term, fully amortized home loan with a relatively small down payment. The buyer paid a small insurance premium to the FHA for a policy that guaranteed to the lender that the agency would pay off the loan and take over the property should the buyer default." Charlotte Allen, "HUD: Who Needs It? Rethinking Federal Housing Policy," *City Journal* (Winter 1994): 6–7, http://www.city-journal.org/printable.php?id=1410, accessed October 29, 2010.

27. Vale, *From the Puritans to the Projects*, 63.

28. Thompson, *A History of HUD*, 5.

29. Ibid.

30. Minneapolis Public Housing Authority, "The History of the Tenant-Based Housing Programs," http://www.mphaonline.org/section8.html, accessed October 29, 2010.

31. Danilo Pelletiere, Michelle Canizio, Morgan Hargrave, and Sheila Crowley, "Housing Assistance for Low Income Households: States Do Not Fill the Gap," National Low Income Housing Coalition (October 2008), http://www2398.ssldomain.com/nlihc/doc/PATCHWORK.pdf, accessed October 29, 2010.

32. Brandt Williams, "Long wait for public housing gets longer," Minnesota Public Radio (June 12, 2008), http://minnesota.publicradio.org/display/web/2008/06/12/housingvoucher/, accessed October 29, 2010.

33. Douglas Rice and Barbara Sard, "The Effects of the Federal Budget Squeeze on Low-Income Housing Assistance," Center on Budget and Policy Priorities (February 1, 2007), 10.

34. The National Association of State and Local Equity Funds, "Creation of the Low Income Housing Tax Credit," http://www.naslef.org/history/, accessed October 29, 2010. By 2007, 300,000 units had already been lost because owners did not renew contracts with HUD to keep rents affordable to low-income renters. Rice and Sard, "The Effects of the Federal Budget Squeeze," 5.

35. U.S. Department of Housing and Urban Development, "About HOPE VI," http://www.hud.gov/offices/pih/programs/ph/hope6/about/, accessed October 29, 2010.

36. Only 7 percent of Cotter/Lang residents were relocated to mixed-income housing in Louisville through HOPE VI, and tracking was haphazard at best. Rick Axtell and Michelle Tooley, "Living in Hope in Kentucky: An Assessment of the Hope VI Redevelopment Project" (paper given at the Society of Christian Ethics, Chicago, January 2009).

37. Rice and Sard, "The Effects of the Federal Budget Squeeze," 9.

38. Roger Lowenstein, "Who Needs the Mortgage-Interest Deduction?" New York Times Magazine, March 5, 2006, http://www.nytimes.com/2006/03/05/magazine/305deduction.1.html, accessed October 29, 2010.

39. United States Department of Housing and Urban Development, "Federal Definition of Homeless," http://portal.hud.gov/portal/page/portal/HUD/topics/homelessness/definition, accessed October 29, 2010.

40. "A Matter of Definition: Responding to Homelessness Among Families, Children, and Youth," http://www.npach.org/newdefinition0725.pdf, accessed October 29, 2010.

41. Rachel L. Swarns, "Capitol Strives to Define 'Homeless,'" New York Times, September 16, 2008, http://www.nytimes.com/2008/09/16/washington/16homeless.htm, accessed October 29, 2010.

42. See "A Matter of Definition" (n. 40, above).

43. Martha R. Burt, Principal Research Associate and Director, Social Services Research Program Urban Institute, "Reauthorization of the McKinney-Vento Homeless Assistance Act," testimony before the U.S. House of Representatives, Committee on Financial Services Subcommittee on Housing and Community Opportunity, October 11, 2007. Full testimony is on Urban Institute website, http://www.urban.org/publications/901120.html, accessed November 23, 2010.

44. 3.8 million more people than the estimated 3.5 million homeless.

45. National Alliance to End Homelessness, "Data Snapshot: Doubled Up in the United States" (March 2008), http://www.endhomelessness.org/content/article/detail/1779, accessed October 29, 2010.

46. "The 2009 Annual Homeless Assessment Report to Congress," Office of Community Planning and Development, U.S. Department of Housing and Urban Development (July 2010), i, http://www.hudhre.info/documents/5thHomelessAssessmentReport .pdf , accessed November 24, 2010.

47. Statistics are based on a 2007 study by the National Law Center on Homelessness and Poverty. "How Many People Experience Homelessness?" National Coalition for the Homeless Fact Sheet (July 2009), http://www.nationalhomeless.org/factsheets/How_Many.html, accessed October 29, 2010.

48. Burt et al., *Helping America's Homeless*, 164–65.

49. HUD's 2006 definition of a chronically homeless person is: "an unaccompanied individual with a disabling condition who has been continuously homeless for a year or more or has experienced four or more episodes of homelessness over the last three years. A disabling condition is defined as a diagnosable substance abuse disorder, serious mental illness, developmental disability, or chronic physical illness or disability, including the co-occurrence of two or more of these conditions." Walter Leginski, "Historical and Contextual Influences on the U.S. Response to Contemporary Homelessness," 2007 National Symposium on Homelessness Research, 11, http://aspe.hhs.gov/hsp/homelessness/symposium07/leginski/index.htm, accessed November 1, 2010.

50. Burt et al., *Helping America's Homeless*, 165.

51. "The Second Annual Homeless Assessment Report to Congress," U.S. Department of Housing and Urban Development, March 2008, iii.

52. Most people who are homeless have incomes one-third of the poverty level. Burt et al., *Helping America's Homeless*, 79.

53. "Who Is Homeless?" National Coalition for the Homeless Fact Sheet (July 2009), http://www.nationalhomeless.org/factsheets/who.html, accessed October 29, 2010.

54. National demographic population of the United States: 74 percent white, 13 percent black, 15 percent Hispanic, 4 percent Asian, 1 percent Native American. "The U.S. Conference of Mayors," *Hunger and Homelessness Survey* (December 2007), 15, http://www.usmayors.org/HHSurvey2007/hhsurvey07.pdf.

55. Ibid.

56. The Department of Veteran Affairs estimates that there are approximately 131,000 homeless veterans. National Alliance to End Homelessness, "Snapshot of Homelessness," http://www.endhomelessness.org/section/about_homelessness/snapshot_of_homelessness#veterans, accessed October 29, 2010.

57. National Alliance to End Homelessness, "Mental Health and Physical Health," http://www.endhomelessness.org/section/issues/mental_physical_health, accessed October 29, 2010; and "The United States Conference of Mayors Hunger and Homelessness Survey" (December 2008), 18.

58. "Who Is Homeless?" (see n. 53, above).

59. Ibid.

60. "Families," National Alliance to End Homelessness, http://www.endhomelessness .org/section/policy/policy_focus_areas/families, accessed October 29, 2010.

61. National Alliance to End Homelessness, "Domestic Violence," http://www.end homelessness.org/section/issues/domestic_violence, accessed October 29, 2010; and "Who Is Homeless?"

62. In 2009, the National Alliance to End Homelessness claimed that around 6 percent of the teenage population (under 18) experiences homelessness at least once. National Alliance to End Homelessness, "Youth," http://www.endhomelessness.org/section /issues/youth, accessed October 29, 2010.

63. "Who Is Homeless?"

64. The Urban Institute, "Five Questions for Martha Burt," http://www.urban.org/ toolkit/fivequestions/MBurt.cfm, accessed November 1, 2010.

65. "Hunger and Homelessness Survey 2007," The United States Conference of Mayors, http://www.usmayors.org/hhsurvey2007/hhsurvey07.pdf, accessed November 1, 2010. Quote from "Addiction Disorders and Homelessness," National Coalition for the Homeless.

66. Burt et al., *Helping America's Homeless*, 98.

67. Marybeth Shinn, "International Homelessness: Policy, Socio-Cultural and Individual Perspectives" *Journal of Social Issues* 63, no. 3 (September 2007): 672.

68. Burt et al., *Helping America's Homeless*, 8.

69. James D. Wright and Beth A. Rubin, "Is Homelessness a Housing Problem?" *Housing Policy Debate* 2, no. 3 (1997): 938.

70. Louis Uchitelle, *The Disposable American: Layoffs and Their Consequences* (New York: Knopf, 2006), 124–50.

71. Mary Elizabeth Hobgood, *Dismantling Privilege: An Ethics of Accountability,* 2nd ed. (Cleveland: Pilgrim, 2009), 94.

72. Uchitelle, *The Disposable American*, 124–50.

73. This is an increase from 46.3 million in 2008. "Income, Poverty and Health Insurance Coverage in the United States: 2009," U.S. Census Bureau News, U.S. Department of Commerce, Washington D.C. (Sept 2010), 22–23; http://www.census.gov/ prod/2010pubs/p60-238.pdf, accessed November 24, 2010.

74. Sharon Parrott and Arloc Sherman, "TANF at 10: Program Results are More Mixed than Often Understood," Washington, D.C.: Center on Budget and Policy Priorities, 2006, http://www.financeproject.org/irc_pubs.cfm?p=24&id=81.

75. "A Plan, Not A Dream: How to End Homelessness in Ten Years," National Alliance to End Homelessness, 21, http://www.endhomelessness.org/content/article/ detail/585, accessed November 1, 2010.

76. "The Facts About Minimum Wage," Center for American Progress, http://www.amer icanprogress.org/pressroom/releases/2007/01/min_wage.html, accessed November 1, 2010.

77. "Before and After Welfare Reform: The Work and Well-Being of Low-Income Single

Parent Families," Institute for Women's Policy Research, June 2003, http://www
.iwpr.org/pdf/D454.pdf, accessed November 1, 2010.

78. "Income, Poverty, and Health Insurance Coverage in the United States: 2009," U.S. Census Bureau News, U.S. Department of Commerce, Washington D.C. (Sept 2010), 5; http://www.census.gov/prod/2010pubs/p60-238.pdf, accessed November 24, 2010.

79. U.S. Department of Housing and Urban Development, "Discrimination in Metropolitan Housing Markets: National Results from Phase 1, Phase 2, and Phase 3 of the Housing Discrimination Study (HDS)," http://www.huduser.org/publications/ hsgfin/msa_sum.html, accessed November 1, 2010.

80. Jane Waldfogel, "The Family Gap for Young Women in the U.S. and Britain," *Journal of Labor Economics* 16 (1998): 507; as quoted in Joan C. Williams and Nancy Segal, "Beyond the Maternal Wall: Relief for Family Caregivers Who Are Discriminated Against On The Job," *Harvard Women's Law Journal* 26 (2003): 77–78.

81. "Extremely low-income households" are 0 to 30 percent of a state's median family income. Danilo Pelletiere, "Preliminary Assessment of American Community Survey Data Shows Housing Affordability Gap Worsened for Lowest Income Households form 2007 to 2008," National Low Income Housing Coalition, Research Note #09-01 (November 30, 2009), 4, http://www.nlihc.org/doc/Prelim-Assess-Rental-Affordability-Gap-State-Level-ACS-12-01.pdf, accessed November 1, 2010.

82. The 30-percent affordability rule was based on a guideline created during the Depression in which a week's wage should cover a month's rent. The guideline was used to ascertain need and eligibility for federal low-income housing policy in 1937. The Brooke Amendment to the Housing and Urban Development Act of 1969 legislated that public housing tenants pay no more than 25 percent of their income for housing. Previous policy set 25 percent as a floor, not a ceiling. Although the 30-percent rule of thumb has been widely used, it is not without its problems as families with children can often afford less than a single person. See Danilo Pelletiere, "Getting to the Heart of Housing's Fundamental Question: How Much Can a Family Afford?" National Low Income Housing Coalition (February 2008), http://www.nlihc.org /doc/AffordabilityResearchNote_2-19-08.pdf, accessed November 1, 2010.

83. "The State of the Nation's Housing 2009," Joint Center for Housing Studies of Harvard University (2009), 26, http://www.jchs.harvard.edu/publications/markets /son2009/son2009.pdf, accessed November 1, 2010.

84. "Households with 'worse case needs' are defined as unassisted renters with very low incomes (below 50% area median income) who pay more than half of their income for housing or live in severely substandard housing." In "Affordable Housing Needs: A Report to Congress on the Significant Need for Housing," Office of Policy Development and Research, U.S. Department of Housing and Urban Development, http:// www.huduser.org/portal/publications/affhsg/affhsgneed.html, accessed November 1, 2010.

85. A majority of these households are fully employed. "Policy Guide 2010," National

Alliance to End Homelessness, http://www.endhomelessness.org/content/article/detail/2462, accessed November 24, 2010.

86. "The State of the Nation's Housing 2009," 26 (see n. 83 above).

87. National Alliance to End Homelessness, "Increase Access to Affordable Housing for Extremely Low Income Families," Federal Policy Brief (December 5, 2009), www.endhomelessness.org/content/general/detail/2597, accessed November 1, 2010.

88. Linda Olsen, Senior Planning and Development Specialist for Domestic Violence and Sexual Assault Prevention Division of the Seattle Human Services Department, "Domestic Violence and Homelessness," PowerPoint presentation, National Conference to End Family Homelessness (February 8, 2008), 2, www.endhomelessness.org/files/1937_file_olsen.ppt, accessed November 1, 2010.

89. "Why Are People Homeless?" National Coalition for the Homeless, http://www.nationalhomeless.org/factsheets/why.html, accessed November 1, 2010.

90. Wright and Rubin, "Is Homelessness a Housing Problem?," 941.

91. Ibid., 943–44.

92. Robert Anderson, National Association of State Alcohol and Drug Abuse Directors, Testimony before the Subcommittee on Health and the Environment, Committee on Commerce, U.S. House of Representatives, August, 1999. From "A Plan, Not A Dream," 22 (see n. 75).

93. National Alliance to End Homelessness, "Homelessness and Prisoner Re-entry," August 11, 2006, http://www.endhomelessness.org/content/article/detail/1082, accessed November 1, 2010.

94. California Department of Corrections, "Prevention Parolee Failure Program: An Evaluation" (Sacramento: California Department of Corrections, 1997), in Caterina Gouvis Roman and Jeremy Travis, *Taking Stock: Housing, Homelessness, and Prisoner Reentry* (Washington, D.C.: Urban Institute, 2004), iv.

95. Jeremy Travis, Amy L. Solomon, and Michelle Waul, *From Prison to Home: The Dimensions and Consequences of Prisoner Reentry* (Washington, D.C.: Urban Institute, 2001), 31–35.

96. In 2004, U.S. incarceration rates by race: whites 393 per 100,000 population; Latinos 957 per 100,000 population; and blacks 2,531 per 100,000 population. Statistics as of June 30, 2004, from *Prison and Jail Inmates at Midyear 2004*, Tables 1, 14, and 15 and U.S. Census (Peter Wagner, June 2005) as found on Prison Policy Initiative Web site http://www.prisonpolicy.org/graphs/raceinc.html. Also see Michael J. Lynch, E. Britt Patterson, and Kristina K. Childs, eds., *Racial Divide: Racial and Ethnic Bias in the Criminal Justice System* (Monsey, N.Y.: Criminal Justice Press, 2008).

97. National Alliance to End Homelessness, "Fundamental Issues to Prevent and End Youth Homelessness" August 10, 2006, 1, http://www.endhomelessness.org/content/article/detail/1058, accessed November 1, 2010.

98. Nan P. Roman and Phyllis Wolfe, "Web of Failure: The Relationship Between Foster Care and Homelessness," National Alliance to End Homelessness, April 1, 1995,

http://www.endhomelessness.org/content/general/detail/1285, accessed November 1, 2010.

99. The number of chronically homeless people dropped by 30 percent in this period from 175,914 to 123,833 (statistics from more than 3,800 cities and counties). Rachel L. Swarns, "U.S. Reports Drop in Homeless Population," *New York Times,* July 30, 2008, http://www.nytimes.com/2008/07/30/us/30homeless.html, accessed November 1, 2010. Other success stories: drop in chronic homelessness by 46 percent over two years in Denver, and by 70 percent in Portland, Oregon. Martha R. Burt, "Reauthorization of the McKinney-Vento Homeless Assistance Act," testimony before the U.S. House of Representatives, Committee on Financial Services Subcommittee on Housing and Community Opportunity, October 11, 2007, 9. http://www.urban.org/publications/901120.html, accessed November 23, 2010.

100. In 1999, Congress told HUD to direct one-third of its funding for homelessness to permanent housing.

101. Leginski, "Historical and Contextual Influences," 10 (see n. 49).

102. "A Plan, Not A Dream," 7 (see n. 75).

103. "Between 1976 and 2004, housing assistance from all federal programs decreased by approximately 48 percent (adjusted for inflation)." "The President's FY 2009 Budget Proposal: Analysis and Policy Implications," PowerPoint presentation, National Alliance to End Homelessness, February 5, 2008, http://www.endhomelessness.org/content/general/detail/1878, accessed November 1, 2010.

104. Rice and Sard, "The Effects of the Federal Budget Squeeze," 1.

105. Linda Couch, "Public Housing," National Low Income Housing Coalition, May 6, 2009, http://www.nlihc.org/detail/article.cfm?article_id=6066&id=19, accessed November 1, 2010; Rice and Sard, "The Effects of the Federal Budget Squeeze," 5.

106. Center for Responsible Lending analysis of 2006 Home Mortgage Disclosure Act data reported by the Federal Financial Institutions Examination Council, as found on the Bread for the World Web site, http://www.bread.org/BFW-Institute/assetbuilding/subprime-loans-foreclosures.html, accessed November 1, 2010.

107. "Record Foreclosure Activity in 2009 Could Have Been Worse," from the RealtyTrac 2009 Year-End U.S. Foreclosure Market Report, http://www.foreclosurepulse.com/blogs/mainblog/archive/2010/01/13/record-foreclosure-activity-in-2009-couldhave-been-worse.aspx, accessed November 1, 2010.

108. The increase of renter households from 2004 to 2007 was over 2 million. "The State of the Nation's Housing 2008," 22 (see n. 83).

109. Danilo Pelletiere, "Renters in Foreclosure: Defining the Problem, Identifying Solutions," National Low Income Housing Coalition (January 2009), http://www.nlihc .org/doc/renters-in-foreclosure.pdf, accessed November 1, 2010.

110. Trymaine Lee, "Families with Children in City Shelters Soar to Record Level," *New York Times,* December 23, 2008, http://www.nytimes.com/2008/12/23/nyregion/23homeless.html, accessed November 1, 2010.

111. Sharon Parrott, "Recession Could Cause Large Increases in Poverty and Push Mil-

lions Into Deep Poverty," Center for Budget and Policy Priorities, November 24, 2008, http://www.cbpp.org/cms/index.cfm?fa=view&id=1290, accessed November 1, 2010.

3. Dominant Ideologies on Housing and Homelessness

1. Cheryl Moch, ed. *Feels Like Home: Fond Remembrances in Words and Pictures* (Chapel Hill: Algonquin Books of Chapel Hill, 1995).

2. "Homeownership and Its Benefits," Urban Policy Brief, no. 2, August 1995, http://www.huduser.org/publications/txt/hdbrf2.txt, accessed November 1, 2010.

3. See Richard K. Green and Michelle J. White, *Measuring the Benefits of Homeowning: Effects on Children* (Chicago: Center for the Study of the Economy and the State, 1994); William M. Rohe and Michael A. Stegman, "The Effects of Homeownership on the Self-Esteem, Perceived Control, and Life Satisfaction of Low-Income People," *Journal of the American Planning Association* 60 (1994): 173–84; Henry G. Cisneros, *Defensible Space: Deterring Crime and Building Community.* (Washington, D.C.: HUD, 1995).

4. Lawrence J. Vale, *From the Puritans to the Projects: Public Housing and Public Neighbors* (Cambridge: Harvard University Press, 2000), 120.

5. Ibid., 121.

6. U.S. Department of Housing and Urban Development Web site, http://archives.hud.gov/initiatives/fbci/topten/topten1.cfm, accessed November 23, 2010.

7. Elizabeth M. Bounds, "Welfare as a Family Value: Conflicting Notions of Family in Protestant Welfare Responses," in *Welfare Policy: Feminist Critiques*, ed. Elizabeth M. Bounds, Pamela K. Brubaker, and Mary E. Hobgood (Cleveland: Pilgrim, 1999), 163.

8. Kathleen R. Arnold, *Homelessness, Citizenship, and Identity: The Uncanniness of Late Modernity* (Albany: State University of New York Press, 2004), 123.

9. This shift happened as the home was no longer the center of productive activity.

10. Todd Depastino, *Citizen Hobo: How a Century of Homelessness Shaped America* (Chicago: University of Chicago Press, 2003), 25.

11. Ibid., 230.

12. Ibid., 229–30.

13. Adolph Reed Jr., "The Underclass as Myth and Symbol: The Poverty of Discourse About Poverty," *Radical America* 24 (1990): 30.

14. The romanticized image of the cottage in rural English villages in the late nineteenth century was a reaction to the perceived ugliness of the Industrial Revolution. Similar, but slightly different, imaging occurred in the United States.

15. Paul Cloke and Rebekah C. Widdowfield, "The Hidden and Emerging Spaces of Rural Homelessness," *Environmental and Planning A* 32, no. 1 (2000): 80.

16. RIS Media Web site: http://www.rismedia.com/wp/2005-02-24/coldwell-banker-system-reports-a-52-percent-increase-in-luxury-sales/, accessed November 1, 2010.

17. In 2006, households in the lowest 60 percent of the income distribution received

only 3 percent of the benefits of the home mortgage interest deduction (HMID), and households in the lowest 80 percent of the income distribution received only 20 percent of the benefits of the HMID. Half of all homeowners do not claim itemized deductions because their mortgage interest is less than the standard deduction, and tenants don't qualify. Information is from the Center for Budget and Policy Priorities.

18. Arnold, *Homelessness, Citizenship, and Identity*, 45.

19. Joseph Betz, "The Homeless Hannah Arendt," in John M. Abbarno, ed., *The Ethics of Homelessness* (Amsterdam: Rodopi, 1999), 220–25.

20. Arnold, *Homelessness, Citizenship, and Identity*, 46–47.

21. Ibid., 126.

22. A stanza from the song "King of the Road." Roger Miller, 1964, *The Return of Roger Miller*, Smash Records.

23. Ken Kyle, *Contextualizing Homelessness: Critical Theory, Homelessness, and Federal Policy Addressing the Homeless* (New York: Routledge, 2005), 64.

24. David Sibley, *Geographies of Exclusion: Society and Difference in the West* (New York: Routledge, 1995), 56–57.

25. Brian J. Walsh and Steven Bouma-Prediger, "With and Without Boundaries: Christian Homemaking amidst Postmodern Homelessness," in *The Hermeneutics of Charity: Interpretation, Selfhood, and Postmodern Faith*, ed. James K. A. Smith and Henry Isaac Venema (Grand Rapids: Brazos, 2004), 232.

26. Sibley, *Geographies of Exclusion*, 57.

27. Stephen Small, "The Contours of Racialization: Structures, Representations, and Resistance in the United States," in *Race, Identity, and Citizenship: A Reader*, ed. Rodolfo D. Torres, Louis F. Mirón, and Jonathan Xavier Inda (Hoboken, N.J.: Blackwell, 1999), 54.

28. A combination of classism and sexism stigmatizes poor single mothers for not fitting into the dominant image of "family" and therefore not upholding "family values." These mothers are blamed for all sorts of "antisocial" and "violent" behavior in poor neighborhoods, and for continuing and teaching a "culture of poverty." Often it is argued that if they would simply get married, all would be well. See William Julius Wilson, *The Truly Disadvantaged: The Inner-City, the Underclass, and Public Policy* (Chicago: University of Chicago Press, 1990); Bounds et al., eds., *Welfare Policy: Feminist Critiques* (Cleveland: Pilgrim, 1999).

29. Reed, "The Underclass as Myth and Symbol," 28.

30. Howard M. Bahr, *Skid Row: An Introduction to Disaffiliation* (New York: Oxford University Press, 1973), 222.

31. Doug A. Timmer, D. Stanley Eitzen, and Kathryn D. Talley, *Paths to Homelessness: Extreme Poverty and the Urban Housing Crisis* (Boulder: Westview, 1994), 14. Howard Bahr argues that the tactic by rehabilitation professionals to have alcoholism accepted as a disease was in part to differentiate a "typical alcoholic" from a "skid row derelict." Bahr, *Skid Row*, 80. See also Reed, "Underclass as Myth and Symbol," 21–40.

32. Arnold, *Homelessness, Citizenship, and Identity*, 91.

33. Bahr, *Skid Row*, 225.

34. "A Continuum of Care is a local or regional system for helping people who are homeless or at imminent risk of homelessness by providing housing and services appropriate to the whole range of homeless needs in the community, from homeless prevention to emergency shelter to permanent housing." Martha R. Burt et al., Urban Institute, "Evaluation of Continuums of Care for Homeless People Final Report," (May 2002), for the Office of Policy Development and Research, U.S. Department of Housing and Urban Development, 3.

35. Amir B. Marvasti, *Being Homeless: Textual and Narrative Constructions* (Lanham, Md.: Lexington, 2003), 9–17.

36. Susan Ruddick, "From the Politics of Homelessness to the Politics of the Homeless," in *Local Places: In the Age of the Global City*, ed. Roger Keil, Gerda R. Wekerle, and David V. J. Bell (Montreal: Black Rose, 1996), 166.

37. Steven V. Roberts, "Reagan on Homelessness: Many Choose to Live in the Streets," *New York Times*, 23 December 1988, http://www.nytimes.com/1988/12/23/us/reagan-on-homelessness-many-choose-to-live-in-the-streets.html, accessed November 29, 2010.

38. Vincent Lyon-Callo, *Inequality, Poverty, and Neoliberal Governance: Activist Ethnography in the Homeless Sheltering Industry* (Peterborough, Ont.: Broadview, 2004), 49–72.

39. Kyle, *Contextualizing Homelessness*, 50–51.

40. Ibid., 44.

41. Ibid.

42. Sibley, *Geographies of Exclusion*, 24–25.

43. Cynthia J. Bogard, *Seasons Such as These: How Homelessness Took Shape in America* (New York: Aldine De Gruyter, 2003), xi–xii.

44. Kyle, *Contextualizing Homelessness*, 50–51.

45. Feldman, *Citizens Without Shelter*, 2.

46. Story of a fifteen-year-old youth. James Garbarino, Janis Wilson, and Anne C. Garbarino, "The Adolescent Runaway," in *Troubled Youth, Troubled Families: Understanding Families At-Risk for Adolescent Maltreatment*, ed. James Garbarino, Cynthia J. Schellenback, Janet Sebes, and Associates (New York: Aldine De Gruyter, 1986), 41. Quoted from Gregg Barak, *Gimme Shelter: A Social History of Homelessness in Contemporary America* (New York: Praeger, 1991), 87.

47. This distinction between the new and old homeless is not new. During the Depression, the new homeless (those who were willing to work, but could not find work) were blameless, while the old homeless were moral degenerates. Arnold, *Homelessness, Citizenship, and Identity*, 91.

48. Timmer et al., *Paths to Homelessness*, 5.

49. Lisa Goodman, Leonard Saxe, and Mary Harvey, "Homelessness as Psychological Trauma: Broadening Perspectives," *American Psychologist* 46, no. 11 (1991): 1222.

50. Ibid.

51. Elliot Liebow, *Tell Them Who I Am: The Lives of Homeless Women* (New York: Free), 25.

52. Marvasti, *Being Homeless*, 53.

53. Feldman, *Citizens Without Shelter*, 96–97.

54. Marvasti, *Being Homeless*, 74.

55. Marvasti argues that although staff members gave different narratives in his interviews with them, he found that even though all of them talked about the complexity of homelessness and noted several structural reasons for homelessness, they all viewed individual failure as the primary source of client problems. He concludes that an emphasis on personal shortcomings is the unifying characteristic of the shelter as a formal organization. Ibid., 89–117.

56. Marvasti notes that there are multiple client narratives of homelessness. The more important point he is making is that homeless clients also interact with the dominant ideologies about homelessness, sometimes rejecting them and other times employing them to achieve particular ends. Ibid., 143–67.

57. Quoted from Lauren Byrne, "Homeless People Share Their Experience During the Third Annual Radio Marathon on Homelessness," in *Spare Change*, January 11–24, 2001; found in Arnold, *Homelessness, Citizenship, and Identity*, 51.

58. See Susan Ruddick, *Young and Homeless in Hollywood: Mapping Social Identities* (New York: Routledge, 1996); Stacey Rowe and Jennifer Wolch, *Social Networks in Time and Space: Homeless Women in Skid Row, Los Angeles* (Los Angeles: Department of Geography, University of Southern California, 1989); Neil Smith, "Homeless/Global: Scaling Places" in *Mapping the Futures: Local Cultures, Global Change*, ed., Jon Bird (London: Routledge, 1993), 87–119; and David Wagner, *Checkerboard Square: Culture and Resistance in a Homelessness Community* (Boulder: Westview, 1993).

59. Ruddick, "From the Politics of Homelessness," in Keil et al., 169.

60. Ibid.

61. Susan Ruddick, "Heterotopias of the Homeless: Strategies and Tactics of Place-making in Los Angeles," *Journal of Theory, Culture, and Politics*. 3, no. 3 (1990): 184–201.

62. David Harvey, "Social Justice, Postmodernism and the City," *International Journal of Urban and Regional Research* 16, no. 4 (1992): 588–601.

63. The Poor People's Economic Human Rights Campaign, a thirty-five-member coalition of workers, welfare, and homeless groups, has organized protest tent cities, petitioned city managers about economic issues facing the poor, and even "met with a UN human rights representative to deliver a report charging the United States government with violating the economic human rights of its poor." Robin Shulman, "Marchers Bring Their Case to UN," *The Village Voice*, November 3–9, 1999, http://www.villagevoice.com/1999-11-02/news/marchers-bring-their-case-to-un/1, accessed November 1, 2010. In Portland, Oregon, a tent city of sixty homeless became "Dignity Village" with its own rules and contributions for electricity, phone

lines, garbage and water, portable toilets, and propane. They now have their own Web site: http://www.dignityvillage.org/, accessed November 26, 2010.

64. Feldman, *Citizens Without Shelter*, 6–7.

65. Kenneth L. Kusmer, *Down and Out, On the Road: The Homeless in American History* (New York: Oxford University Press, 2002), 27.

66. Bahr, *Skid Row*, 224.

67. Kusmer, *Down and Out, On the Road*, 43–52.

68. Ibid., 92.

69. Ibid., vii.

70. Sibley, *Geographies of Exclusion*, 56.

71. National Coalition for the Homeless, "A Dream Denied: The Criminalization of Homelessness in U.S. Cities," http://www.nationalhomeless.org/publications/crim report/meanestcities.html, accessed November 1, 2010.

72. Feldman, *Citizens Without Shelter*, 30.

73. Eric Brosch, "No Place Like Home: Orlando's Poor Laws Attempt to Regulate the Homeless Away, *Harpers* 296 (April 1998): 58; quote taken from Kyle, *Contextualizing Homelessness*, 101.

74. Feldman, *Citizens Without Shelter*, 38.

75. Between 2005 and 2007, attacks increased by 65 percent. In Florida, the problem was so severe that the National Coalition for the Homeless set up speakers bureaus to address youth who see attacking the homeless as a sport. Amy Green, "Attacks on the Homeless Rise, With Youths Mostly to Blame," *New York Times*, February 15, 2008, http://www.nytimes.com/2008/02/15/us/15homeless.html, accessed November 1, 2010.

76. Bogard, *Seasons Such as These*, 198.

77. Marvasti, *Being Homeless*, 30.

78. There are also many providers who support the "Housing First" strategy. I am not arguing for or against Housing First, but am simply pointing out that some who are involved in the treatment end of the homeless seem to be against this move toward housing people before receiving therapy or other types of assistance. There are valid arguments for and against the Housing First policy, and I doubt there is one plan that fits all.

79. Lyon-Callo, *Inequality, Poverty, and Neoliberal Governance*, 12.

80. Ibid., 13.

81. Arnold, *Homelessness, Citizenship, and Identity*, 96.

82. George Todd, "A Reformed Perspective on Faith-Based Initiatives: How do we apply our theology to charitable choice?," *Church & Society*, Presbyterian Church (U.S.A.), (May/June 2001), 77.

83. Kyle, *Contextualizing Homelessness*, 63–107.

84. *New York Times*, September 27, 1981, as quoted in Jennifer Wolch, *The Shadow State: Government and Voluntary Sector in Transition* (New York: The Foundation Center, 1990), 5.

85. Wolch, *The Shadow State*, 5.

86. Ibid.

87. Emilie M. Townes, "Welfare in the Age of Spectacles," in Bounds et al., eds., *Welfare Policy*, 228.

88. Heather Beth Johnson, *The American Dream and the Power of Wealth: Choosing Schools and Inheriting Inequality in the Land of Opportunity* (New York: Routledge, 2006), 24.

89. Ibid., 130.

90. Ibid., 31.

91. Ibid., 21.

92. She is referring specifically to white privilege in this article, but her analogy can apply to all of the unearned privileges dominant groups have. Peggy McIntosh, "White Privilege: Unpacking the Invisible Knapsack," in *The Meaning of Difference: American Constructions of Race, Sex and Gender, Social Class, Sexual Orientation, and Disability*, ed. Karen Roseblum and Toni-Michelle C. Travis, 5th ed. (New York: McGraw-Hill, 2008), 368.

93. See "10 Rags to Riches Billionaires," *Smart Money Daily* Web site, July 10, 2008, http://www.smartmoneydaily.com/celeb-finance/10-rags-to-riches-billionaires. aspx, accessed November 1, 2010.

94. G. William Domhoff, University of California at Santa Cruz, "Wealth, Income, and Power" (April 2010), http://sociology.ucsc.edu/whorulesamerica/power/wealth. html, accessed November 1, 2010.

95. In 2007, the top 1 percent owned 34.6 percent of all wealth, while the bottom 80 percent owned 15 percent of all wealth. See ibid.

96. James B. Davies, "Wealth and Economic Inequality," in *New Oxford Handbook of Economic Inequality*, ed. Wiemer Salverda, Brian Nolan, and Timothy M. Smeeding (New York: Oxford University Press, 2009), 144.

4. Rescue and Recovery Response

1. Stephen Burger, "Arise, Take Up Thy Mat, and Walk," *Policy Review* 79 (September/October 1996): 22.

2. Conversation with woman at lunch, January 12, 2009, Association of Gospel Rescue Missions affiliate (hereafter AGRM). All conversations and interviews in this chapter are with Laura Stivers.

3. Evangelicalism is a Protestant Christian movement that sees a need for a personal conversion to belief in Jesus Christ (being "born again"), has a high regard for biblical authority, emphasizes the death and resurrection of Jesus, and strongly promotes making an effort to live the gospel in one's life. Fundamentalist Christianity, a conservative subset of evangelicalism, advocates inerrancy of the Bible.

4. "AGRM History, Time to Reflect, and Look Ahead," Association of Gospel Rescue Missions, http://www.agrm.org/i4a/pages/Index.cfm?pageID=3312;%20accessed% 206/14/09, accessed November 21, 2010.

5. Simply shelter without programs to seriously address addiction (e.g., two meals and a bed).

6. Their twelve-step program stems from Alcoholics Anonymous, but is biblically based. They use the Serenity text, an explanation of the twelve steps in conjunction with books from the New Testament. See Robert Hemfelt and Richard Fowler, *Serenity: A Companion for Twelve Step Recovery* (Nashville: Thomas Nelson, 1990).

7. See http://www.agrm.org/i4a/pages/index.cfm?pageid=3604 for AGRM's statement of faith, accessed November 21, 2010.

8. My observations come from my time spent at each mission, and through serving in mission soup kitchens and attending seasonal parties for families in transitional housing.

9. At all of the affiliates I visited, the clients were referred to as "guests."

10. His point in saying this was that faith helps him to know and love these people. Staff interview, February 27, 2009, AGRM affiliate.

11. Guest interviews, January 12 and 16, 2009, AGRM affiliate.

12. 2005 Annual Report, Charlotte Rescue Mission, Charlotte, North Carolina.

13. 2007 Charlotte Rescue Mission Web site. Recently they changed their mission statement, placing a stronger emphasis on addiction over homelessness: "To minister the Good News of Christianity to individuals caught in the cycles of poverty, hopelessness, and chemical addictions by meeting their spiritual, physical, social, psychological, and vocational needs." http://charlotterescuemission.org/about/, accessed November 23, 2010.

14. Charlotte Rescue Mission brochure, 2007.

15. Burger, "Arise, Take Up Thy Mat, and Walk," 24. While this article is dated, most executive directors I spoke to claimed 60 to 70 percent of the homeless have addictions to drugs and/or alcohol.

16. Staff interview, February 27, 2009, AGRM affiliate.

17. Staff interview, June 28, 2007, AGRM affiliate.

18. Staff interview, January 12, 2009, AGRM affiliate.

19. Ibid.

20. "Whether effects of mental or physical abuse or simply poor choices led clients on a course of self-destruction, the staff at the New Life Program endeavor to help them understand how the love of Jesus Christ can redeem their lives." Tacoma Rescue Mission 2006–2007 Annual Report.

21. Staff interview, January 14, 2009, AGRM affiliate.

22. Charlotte Rescue Mission brochure, 2007.

23. "Master's Touch" brochure, Wayside Cross Ministries, 2008.

24. "A Changed Life: The Testimony of Luke Money," *News and Views for Vision*, Winston-Salem Rescue Mission, Winter 2007.

25. Male guest in addiction program interview, January 12, 2009, AGRM affiliate.

26. Female guest in addiction program interview, July 25, 2007, AGRM affiliate.

27. Ibid.

28. "Sandi B. sees herself as a survivor, not a victim," *The Beacon: The Newsletter of Charlotte Rescue Mission* (Holiday 2006).

29. For one Rescue Mission, breaking the cycle of homelessness and poverty is its vision statement and motto, http://www.opendoormission.org/about, accessed November 24, 2010.

30. Such patterns in generational poverty include: money is to be spent not saved; matriarchal structure; oral language tradition; survival orientation; lover/fighter role for men; rescuer/martyr role for women; belief in fate; polarized thinking; present time orientation; and lack of organization. Ruby K. Payne, Philip E. DeVol, and Terie Dreussi Smith, *Bridges Out of Poverty: Strategies for Professionals and Communities* (Highlands, Tex.: aha! Process, Inc., 2006).

31. Staff interview, January 12, 2009, AGRM affiliate.

32. Staff interview, February 27, 2009, AGRM affiliate.

33. Some staff I spoke to did not eliminate economic factors from the picture. One program director differentiated between types of homelessness. He said the chronically homeless are usually dealing with chemical dependency and/or mental illness. Others, he claimed, are homeless due to low-paying jobs with no social-support network. The staff at one women's shelter acknowledged economic factors, such as lack of affordable housing and lack of social supports, but claimed that the main causes of homelessness are substance abuse and mental health issues.

34. Burger, "Arise, Take Up Thy Mat, and Walk," 23.

35. Staff interview, June 28, 2007, AGRM affiliate.

36. "Jerry's Story" Raleigh Rescue Mission, http://www.raleighrescue.org/content/jeremys-story, accessed November 24, 2010.

37. Staff interview, February 27, 2009, AGRM affiliate.

38. Staff interview, January 14, 2009, AGRM affiliate.

39. Staff interview, June 28, 2007, AGRM affiliate.

40. "A Changed Life: The Testimony of Luke Money."

41. Staff interview, January 14, 2009, AGRM affiliate.

42. Staff interview, January 14, 2009, AGRM affiliate.

43. "From Prison to Praise: My Journey from Drug Addiction to Faith in Christ," *MorningStar Chronicle* (Holiday 2008), MorningStar Mission Ministries, Inc.

44. As one staff person said, "None of us deserves anything. We only deserve hellfire and brimstone. Grace is about receiving something we don't deserve. Ministry of grace is not because we deserve it, but because of God's mercy." Ibid.

45. Charlotte Rescue Mission, "With God's Help" video, http://www.youtube.com/watch?v=Lr-AJt5U-aE, accessed November 24, 2010.

46. Female guest in addiction program interview, June 25, 2007, AGRM affiliate.

47. Staff interview, June 21, 2007, AGRM affiliate.

48. Staff interview, February 27, 2009, AGRM affiliate.

49. Staff interviews, June 18 and 21 2007, AGRM affiliate.

50. Charlotte Rescue Mission, http://charlotterescuemission.org/about/, accessed November 24, 2010.

51. Staff interview, June 21, 2007, AGRM affiliate.

52. Staff interview, February 27, 2009, AGRM affiliate.

53. Staff interview, January 12, 2009, AGRM affiliate.

54. Ibid.

55. Guest in addiction program interview, July 25, 2007, AGRM affiliate.

56. Staff interview AGRM, February 27, 2009, AGRM affiliate.

57. Guest in family shelter interview, January 12, 2009, AGRM affiliate.

58. Stephen Burger, "Viewpoint: The Changing Face of Despair: A Call to Action," Association of Gospel Rescue Missions, *The Calling* (October 1999).

59. Staff interview, February 27, 2009, AGRM affiliate.

60. Guest in family shelter interview, January 12, 2009, AGRM affiliate.

61. Female guest in addiction program interview, July 25, 2007, AGRM affiliate.

62. "Denver Downtown Partnership Award" video, Denver Rescue Mission, http://www.denverrescuemission.org/media.html, accessed November 2, 2010.

63. He said also that a third of the mission's budget comes from the mission's thrift store, which is run mainly by the clients. Staff interview, June 28, 2007, AGRM affiliate. On another note, AGRM retired executive director Stephen Burger opposed requiring that homeless men and women who do work as part of rehabilitation should be considered employees under the Fair Labor Standards Act. He disagreed with the 1990 Labor Department determination that the Salvation Army pay minimum wage to clients performing work as part of rehabilitation. The Labor Department never enforced this ruling. Burger, "Arise, Take Up Thy Mat, and Walk," 26.

64. This director believed that lack of discipline was due to no father figure in the lives of the male guests at his mission. They had no one to discipline them or to serve as an example. This lack of a family unit, in his opinion, is why these men got involved in gangs, smoking, alcohol, and drugs at a young age. He said, "Ages twelve to eighteen are formative years. They have no father figure for discipline and all of a sudden they wake up at forty to fifty years old with poor decision-making skills and a lack of education." Staff interview, June 28, 2007, AGRM affiliate.

65. Burger, "Arise, Take Up Thy Mat, and Walk," 25.

66. Burger, "Viewpoint: The Changing Face of Despair" (see n. 58).

67. Staff interview, January 12, 2009, AGRM affiliate.

68. Marcus, "I Found a True Relationship with God," *The Beacon: The Newsletter of Charlotte Rescue Mission* (February/March 2007): 3.

69. Female guest in addiction program interview, July 25, 2007, AGRM affiliate.

70. Staff interview, June 28, 2007, AGRM affiliate.

71. Staff interview, January 14, 2009, AGRM affiliate.

72. Staff interview, February 27, 2009, AGRM affiliate.

73. Staff interview, January 14, 2009, AGRM affiliate.

74. Until 2010 there was a list of affiliates and executive directors on the national Web

site of AGRM that illustrated the overwhelmingly male leadership. Currently there is a list of AGRM District Officers that demonstrates male leadership: http://www .agrm.org/i4a/pages/index.cfm?pageid=3364, accessed November 24, 2010.

75. Most affiliates did not give me specific demographics, but for most missions, more than half the guests are African American, and the Hispanic population is increasing.

76. Faculty of City Vision College, http://www.cityvision.edu/cms/cv/faculty-and-staff, accessed November 2, 2010.

77. Staff interviews, June 18, 21, and 28, 2007, AGRM affiliates.

78. *Addressing Immorality*, produced by The Women and Family Track of the Association of Gospel Rescue Missions.

79. Staff interview, June 21, 2007, AGRM affiliate.

80. Staff interview, January 14, 2009, AGRM affiliate.

81. When I asked why there are more blacks than whites in programs when whites do not see avoidance of shame as a cultural value either, he did not really have a response. Ibid.

5. Low-Income Homeownership Response

1. Millard Fuller, quoted in Jonathan T. M. Reckford, *Creating a Habitat for Humanity: No Hands but Yours* (Minneapolis: Fortress Press, 2007), 46.

2. Staff interview, February 18, 2009, Habitat for Humanity International affiliate (hereafter HHI). All interviews are by Laura Stivers.

3. There are another 550 international affiliates; see http://www.habitat.org/how/ affiliates.aspx, accessed November 3, 2010.

4. See Jerome P. Baggett, *Habitat for Humanity: Building Private Homes, Building Public Religion* (Philadelphia: Temple University Press, 2001).

5. "The History of Habitat," http://www.habitat.org/how/historytext.aspx. They expect to build over 400,000 by 2011. "Introducing Habitat" video, http://www.habitat.org/ videogallery/default.aspx. Both accessed November 3, 2010.

6. Millard Fuller with Diane Scott, *No More Shacks! The Daring Vision of Habitat for Humanity* (Waco, Texas: Word, 1986), 20.

7. Staff interview, June 14, 2007, HHI affiliate.

8. Staff interview, August 8, 2007, HHI affiliate; "Myths (and Facts) About Habitat for Humanity," http://www.habitat.org/how/myths.aspx.

9. 2010 HUD Area Median Incomes, U.S. Department for Housing and Urban Development, https://www.efanniemae.com/sf/refmaterials/hudmedinc/.

10. My student assistant, Jonathan M. Smith, and I participated in a number of Habitat builds, and attended at least one home dedication.

11. I am aware, however, that I have imposed my worldview by which themes I chose to emphasize.

12. Millard Fuller, *More Than Houses: How Habitat for Humanity Is Transforming Lives and Neighborhoods* (Nashville: Word, 2000), 18.

13.   Ibid., 31–52.

14.   "Why Habitat for Humanity Is Needed," http://www.habitat.org/how/why.aspx, accessed November 3, 2010.

15.   Henry G. Cisneros, Jack F. Kemp, Nicolas P. Retinas, and Ken W. Colton, *Opportunity and Progress: A Bipartisan Platform for National Housing Policy* (Cambridge, Mass.: Joint Center for National Housing Studies of Harvard University, 2006), 4; as cited in Reckford, *Creating a Habitat for Humanity*, 47.

16.   "Why Habitat for Humanity Is Needed" (see n. 14).

17.   Staff interview, January 15, 2009, HHI affiliate.

18.   Fuller, *More Than Houses*, 31.

19.   "Mom Seizes a Better Life," *Habitat World* (January 2005), Habitat for Humanity International, http://www.habitat.org/hw/dec-jan05/feature3a.html, accessed November 23, 2010.

20.   Staff interview, February 18, 2009, HHI affiliate.

21.   Before moving into their Habitat home, they lived in a two-bedroom apartment with ten children. Ibid.

22.   "Mom Seizes a Better Life for Herself and Her Daughters," *Habitat World* (January 2005), Habitat for Humanity International, http://www.habitat.org/hw/dec-jan05/feature3.html, accessed November 23, 2010.

23.   "New York: Healthier and Happier in a Habitat House," *Habitat World* (December 2008), http://www.habitat.org/hw/dec_2008/feature3d.html, accessed November 3, 2010.

24.   "Freedom to Thrive," Habitat for Humanity International Homeowner Stories, http://www.habitat.org/faces_places/hom/devoss.aspx#P0_0, accessed November 3, 2010.

25.   Staff interview, February 18, 2009, HHI affiliate.

26.   "North Carolina: A Homeowner's Experience—in Her Own Words," *Habitat World* (December 2008), http://www.habitat.org/hw/dec_2008/feature3c.html, accessed November 3, 2010.

27.   Staff interview, January 15, 2009, HHI affiliate.

28.   Fuller, *More Than Houses*, 38.

29.   Ibid., 40.

30.   Staff interview, February 18, 2009, HHI affiliate.

31.   Ibid.

32.   Staff interview, January 15, 2009, HHI affiliate.

33.   Ibid.

34.   "Faces and Places—Homeowner Stories," http://www.habitat.org/faces_places/hom/list.aspx, accessed November 3, 2010.

35.   Fuller, *More Than Houses*, 107.

36.   Ibid., 1.

37.   Paul Leonard, *Music of a Thousand Hammers: Inside Habitat for Humanity* (New York: Continuum, 2006), 48.

38. Anna Wilson, "A House, A Home," http://www.habitat.org/videogallery/psa.aspx ?print=true, accessed November 23, 2010.

39. Homeowner interview, March 23, 2009, HHI affiliate.

40. Homeowner interview, March 25, 2009, HHI affiliate.

41. Fuller, *More Than Houses*, 53.

42. Ibid., 56.

43. Homeowner interview, March 23, 2009, HHI affiliate.

44. Fuller, *More Than Houses*, 54.

45. Staff interview, August 8, 2007, HHI affiliate.

46. Staff interview, June 14, 2007, HHI affiliate.

47. One executive director I spoke to said his committee did not have a matrix for determining applicants' "willingness to partner." He said it mainly comes down to the applicants' attitudes in conversation. Two other factors for this director are whether the applicants have a home church and if they are involved in the community. Staff interview, June 14, 2007, HHI affiliate.

48. Baggett says that 76 percent of families using public housing are female-headed, while only one-third of Habitat families are. Baggett, *Habitat for Humanity*, 244.

49. Staff interview, August 8, 2007, HHI affiliate.

50. Staff interview, January 15, 2009, HHI affiliate.

51. Staff interview, March 25, 2009, HHI affiliate.

52. Tom Hall, "The Economics of Jesus," in *Kingdom Building for the 21st Century: Voices form the Soul of Habitat for Humanity* (Americus, Ga.: Habitat for Humanity, 2006), 56.

53. Current executive director Jonathan Reckford lists five root causes of poverty, the first being family history, with an emphasis on the culture of dependency that develops. Even when he lists oppression as a factor, he writes, "Poverty occurs in some societies when one group that is in power chooses to dominate and exploit another." This quotation emphasizes individual, not institutional, oppression. In other words, Reckford does not note that capitalism itself might be oppressive. Reckford, *Creating a Habitat for Humanity*, 51–59.

54. Clarence Jordan, "A Personal Letter from Clarence Jordan to Friends of Koinonia," in *Kingdom Building for the 21st Century*, 12.

55. Fuller, *More Than Houses*, 52.

56. Fuller, *No More Shacks*, 15.

57. Staff interview, January 14, 2009, HHI affiliate.

58. Leonard, *Music of a Thousand Hammers*, 11.

59. Homeowner interview, March 25, 2009, HHI affiliate.

60. Fuller, *No More Shacks*, 127.

61. Staff interview, January 14, 2009, HHI affiliate.

62. Hall, "The Economics of Jesus," in *Kingdom Building for the 21st Century*, 59.

63. Homeowner interview, March 23, 2009, HHI affiliate.

64. Millard Fuller, "Building the Kingdom of God," in *Kingdom Building for the 21st Century*, 31.

65. Fuller, *No More Shacks*, 18.

66. Clive Rainey, "Partnership—the Heart of Habitat for Humanity," in *Kingdom Building for the 21st Century*, 6.

67. Sam Emerick, "Principles That Undergird the Habitat Movement," in ibid., 15.

68. Fuller, "Building the Kingdom of God," in ibid., 31.

69. Baggett, *Habitat for Humanity*, 51.

70. Ibid., 53.

71. "Whirlpool Employees Find 'Something Special and Personal' on 200,000th Build Site," Habitat for Humanity International Volunteer Stories, http://www.habitat.org/faces_places/vol/whirlpool.aspx#P0_0, accessed November 3, 2010.

72. Baggett, *Habitat for Humanity*, 134.

73. "From Tragedy Springs Hope," Habitat for Humanity International Homeowner Stories, http://www.habitat.org/faces_places/hom/from_tragedy_springs_hope .aspx#P0_0, accessed November 3, 2010.

74. "Sacrifice for a Season," Habitat for Humanity International Homeowner Stories, http://www.habitat.org/faces_places/hom/Burt.aspx#P0_0, accessed November 3, 2010.

75. "Following Good Advice," Habitat for Humanity International Homeowner Stories, http://www.habitat.org/faces_places/hom/Eirhart.aspx#P0_0, accessed November 3, 2010.

76. Baggett, *Habitat for Humanity*, 107–8.

77. Reckford, *Creating a Habitat for Humanity*, 55–56.

78. "On the Roof with God," Habitat for Humanity International, http://www.habitat .org/disaster/stories/08_20_2007_reese_family.aspx?print=true, accessed November 23, 2010.

79. Reckford, *Creating a Habitat for Humanity*, 63–67.

80. Fuller, *No More Shacks*, 21.

81. *Habitat World* (December 1984), 3; quoted in Baggett, *Habitat for Humanity*, 53.

82. As quoted on the Habitat for Humanity, International, Web site "A Life Changed by God": "From humble beginnings in Alabama, Millard Fuller rose to become a young, self-made millionaire. A graduate of Auburn University in Auburn, Ala., and the University of Alabama Law School at Tuscaloosa, he and a college friend began a marketing firm while still in school. Fuller's business expertise and entrepreneurial drive made him a millionaire at age 29. But as the business prospered, his health, integrity and marriage suffered. These crises prompted Fuller to re-evaluate his values and direction. His soul-searching led to reconciliation with his wife and to a renewal of his Christian commitment. The Fullers then took a drastic step: They decided to sell all of their possessions, give the money to the poor and begin searching for a new focus for their lives." http://www.habitat.org/how/millard.aspx, accessed November 3, 2010.

83. Staff interview, August 8, 2007, HHI affiliate.

84. Fuller, *No More Shacks*, 190.

85. Jordan, "A Personal Letter," in *Kingdom Building for the 21st Century*, 12.

86. Fuller, *No More Shacks*, 71.
87. Ibid., 119.
88. Jonathan Reckford, "Answering God's Call to Action," in *Kingdom Building for the 21st Century*, 44–46.
89. Jill Claflin, "Habitat for Humanity's Mission Principles," in ibid., 80.
90. Shawn Reeves, "Transformation of Reconciliation," in ibid., 36.
91. Fuller, *No More Shacks*, 127.
92. Ibid.
93. Staff interviews, June 14, 2007; January 15, 2009; February 18, 2009, HHI affiliates.
94. Claflin, "Habitat for Humanity's Mission Principles," in *Kingdom Building for the 21st Century*, 79.
95. "Why Advocacy," in ibid., 85–88.

6. Prophetic-Disruption Assessment and Response

1. National Coalition for the Homeless, "How Many People Experience Homelessness?" fact sheet, http://www.nationalhomeless.org/publications/facts/How_Many .pdf, accessed November 8, 2010.
2. This statement is based on comments from executive directors. Habitat for Humanity does not have data on tenure of Habitat homeowners.
3. Herbert J. Gans, *The War Against the Poor: The Underclass and Antipoverty Policy* (New York: Basic, 1995), 83.
4. Female client, interview by Laura Stivers, July 25, 2007, Association of Gospel Rescue Missions affiliate.
5. Gans, *The War Against the Poor*, 59–65.
6. Ibid., 66–68.
7. Joseph Barndt, *Understanding and Dismantling Racism: The Twenty-First Century Challenge to White America* (Minneapolis: Fortress Press, 2007), 78–79.
8 Twenty percent of homeless youth are lesbian, gay, bisexual, transgender, and/or queer (a conservative estimate). One cause is rejection and forcible eviction from their homes due to their sexual orientation, but usually the causes are multiple, including poverty, family conflict, abuse, and disabilities. National Alliance to End Homelessness, "The Incidence and Vulnerability of LGBTQ Homeless Youth," Youth Homelessness Series Brief no. 2 (December 8, 2008), http://www.endhomelessness. org/content/article/detail/2141, accessed November 8, 2010.
9. They were constrained in part by the cost of land, but their cookie-cutter model of small plots for houses is also based on a particularly American suburbia model of housing. Homeowner interview, by Laura Stivers, March 23, 2009, Habitat for Humanity International affiliate.
10. This affiliate did a great job of accommodating this family, but it was clear that there was no precedent for such a house. Homeowner interview, by Laura Stivers, March 25, 2009, Habitat for Humanity International affiliate.
11. Howard Karger, "The Home Ownership Myth," *Dollars & Sense: The Magazine of Economic Justice* 270 (Spring 2007): 15.

12. Carolina Katz Reid, "Achieving the American Dream? A Longitudinal Analysis of the Homeownership Experience of Low-Income Households" (Ph.D. dissertation, department of geography, University of Washington, 2004), cited in ibid.

13. The most recent data I found was a study by Donald Haurin and Stuart Rosenthal. They use a less restrictive definition of low-income buyer than Reid and claim that, from 1979 through 2000, 43 percent of low-income buyers did not keep their homes for more than five years compared to 30 percent of high-income buyers. Donald R. Haurin and Stuart S. Rosenthal, *The Growth of Earnings of Low-Income Households and the Sensitivity of Their Homeownership Choices to Economic and Socio-Demographic Shocks*, United States Department of Housing and Urban Development, Office of Policy Development and Research (2005). Cited in Christopher E. Herbert and Eric S. Belsky, "The Homeownership Experience of Low-Income and Minority Households: A Review and Synthesis of the Literature," *Cityscape: A Journal of Policy Development and Research* 10, no. 2 (2008), United States Department of Housing and Urban Development, http://www.huduser.org/periodicals/cityscpe /vol10num2/ch1.pdf, 14, accessed November 8, 2010.

14. Herbert and Belsky, "Homeownership Experience of Low-Income and Minority Households."

15. Joe Sims, "The End of Neo-Liberalism and Bush's Last Scam: How Racism Sparked the Financial Crisis," *Political Affairs Magazine* (January 28, 2009): 6.

16. Ibid., 7.

17. See David Cay Johnston, *Free Lunch: How the Wealthiest Americans Enrich Themselves at Government Expense (And Stick You With the Bill)*, reprint ed. (New York: Portfolio Trade, 2008); and resources at United For a Fair Economy Web site, http:// www.faireconomy.org/tags/reports, accessed November 8, 2010.

18. Jerome P. Baggett, *Habitat for Humanity: Building Private Homes, Building Public Religion* (Philadelphia: Temple University Press, 2001), 103–38.

19. See the chapter "The Economics of Jesus," in Millard Fuller with Diane Scott, *Love in the Mortar Joints: The Story of Habitat for Humanity* (Clinton, N.J: New Win, 1980), 85–99.

20. The ouster of founder Millard Fuller from Habitat in 2005 coincided with a more corporate way of running Habitat and more emphasis being placed on Habitat's name status over its grassroots identity. See Bettie B. Youngs, *The House That Love Built: The Story of Millard and Linda Fuller, Founders of Habitat for Humanity and The Fuller Center for Housing* (Charlottesville, Va.: Hampton Roads, 2007).

21. Baggett, *Habitat for Humanity*, 172–73.

22. Jennifer R. Wolch, *The Shadow State: Government and Voluntary Sector in Transition* (New York: The Foundation Center, 1990), 41.

23. Ibid., 42.

24. Traci C. West, *Disruptive Christian Ethics: When Racism and Women's Lives Matter* (Louisville: Westminster John Knox, 2006), 52.

25. Ibid., 54.

7. A Home for All in God's Just and Compassionate Community

1. Interview with Bill Kirlin-Hackett, director of Interfaith Task Force on Homelessness, Seattle, Washington, by Laura Stivers, April 21, 2009.

2. Rita Nakashima Brock and Rebecca Ann Parker use the terms *ethical* and *grace* together to "suggest that the idea of paradise carries both the grace of the core goodness of life on earth, and humanity's responsibility for sustaining it." See Brock and Parker, *Saving Paradise: How Christianity Traded Love of This World for Crucifixion and Empire* (Boston: Beacon, 2008), 29.

3. Ibid.

4. Craig Rennebohm with David Paul, *Souls in the Hands of a Tender God: Stories of the Search for Home and Healing on the Street.* (Boston: Beacon, 2008), 163.

5. Ibid., 175.

6. The ideas on hospitality as justice were first developed in a section I wrote for the homelessness document of the Presbyterian Church (U.S.A), *From Homelessness to Hope: Constructing Just, Sustainable Communities For All God's People*, adopted by General Assembly, June 2008.

7. Antonio Machado, *Times Alone: Selected Poems of Antonio Machado*, trans. Robert Bly (Middletown, Conn.: Wesleyan University Press, 1983), 109. Bill Kirlin-Hackett, director of the Interfaith Task Force on Homelessness, referred me to this poem.

8. Charles Tilly, *Social Movement 1768–2004* (Boulder: Paradigm, 2004), 16–37.

9. Ibid., 3–4.

10. Ibid., 35.

11. Qualifying families can receive a government voucher that subsidizes the cost of renting a place to live. Families pay 30 percent of the rent, and the fair market rental price in their geographic area limits the amount of the voucher.

12. See the Web site of Good Jobs First for ways that communities have held corporations accountable; http://www.goodjobsfirst.org, accessed November 8, 2010.

13. "Proposed military spending for 2009 is over $515 billion. This is the eleventh year of continuous increases in the base military budget and does not include a supplemental package of $70 billion for war in the Middle East. The Iraq war alone costs 10 billion a month (or $720 million a day or $50,000 a minute) in taxpayer's money. . . . in 2007 the federal budget eliminated or reduced 141 social programs and cut non-security discretionary spending by over $2 billion." Mary Elizabeth Hobgood, *Dismantling Privilege: An Ethics of Accountability*, 2nd ed. (Cleveland: Pilgrim, 2009), 90–91.

14. Reinhold Niebuhr, *Moral Man and Immoral Society* (New York: Charles Scribner's Sons, 1960), 21.

15. Martin Luther King Jr., "The Strength to Love," in *A Testament of Hope: The Essential Writings of Martin Luther King, Jr.*, ed. James M. Washington (San Francisco: HarperCollins, 1986), 492.

16. Interview with Bill Kirlin-Hackett, April 21, 2009.

17. Interview with Paul Christie, former executive director of Hands on Hartford, Hartford, Connecticut, by Laura Stivers, May 5, 2009.

18. Peter Dreier, "Community Organizing for What? Progressive Politics and Movement Building in America," in *Transforming the City: Community Organizing and the Challenge of Political Change*, ed. Marion Orr (Lawrence: University Press of Kansas, 2007), 218–51.

19. Interview with Bill Kirlin-Hackett, April 21, 2009.

20. Marjaleena Repo, "Organising 'the Poor'—Against the Working Class," *Transformation* 1, no. 2 (March/April 1971): 4–15.

21. "Core Values," Glide Memorial United Methodist Church, http://www.glide.org/page.aspx?pid=406, accessed November 8, 2010.

22. "History of Glide," Glide Memorial United Methodist Church, http://www.glide.org/page.aspx?pid=412, accessed November 8, 2010.

23. St. Leo's Church, Tacoma, Washington, http://www.stleoparish.org/ministries/justice.htm, accessed November 8, 2010.

24. Emanuel Lutheran Church, story related in e-mail interaction with Paul Christie, April 29, 2009.

25. "Faces of Homelessness: A Manual," National Coalition for the Homeless, http://www.nationalhomeless.org/faces/faces_manual.pdf, accessed November 8, 2010.

26. Steinbruck Center for Urban Studies, http://www.lutherplace.org/steinbruckcenter/, accessed November 8, 2010.

27. Lutheran Volunteer Corps, http://www.lutheranvolunteercorps.org/template/index.cfm, accessed November 8, 2010.

28. Sojourners Annual Report 2007, Sojourners, http://www.sojo.net/about_us/2007_Annual_Report.pdf, accessed November 8, 2010.

29. Ibid.

30. Sojourners, "Why Focus on Poverty?," http://www.sojo.net/index.cfm?action=events.M2EP&item=M2EP-policy-page#why, accessed November 29, 2010.

31. Silver Spring Interfaith Housing Coalition, http://www.ssihc.org, accessed November 8, 2010.

32. Churches United for the Homeless, http://www.churches-united.org, accessed November 8, 2010.

33. Hands on Hartford, http://www.handsonhartford.org, accessed November 8, 2010.

34. HOPE Gardens, http://www.unc.edu/campusyhope/Hope_Gardens.html, accessed November 8, 2010.

35. Rebecca Putterman, "Junior's HOPE Garden to Help the Homeless," *Daily Tar Heel*, August 31, 2009, http://www.dailytarheel.com/index.php/article/2009/08/juniors_hope_garden_to_help_the_homeless, accessed November 8, 2010.

36. The Sullivan Center, http://thesullivancenter.org/index.php/sullivan/, accessed November 8, 2010.

37. Della Spearman, interview by Laura Stivers, May 19, 2010.

38. The Interfaith Task Force on Homelessness, http://itfhomeless.org/, accessed November 8, 2010.

39. Metro Interfaith Coalition for Affordable Housing, http://www.micah.org/, accessed November 8, 2010.

40. "History," PICO National Network, http://www.piconetwork.org/about?id=0006, accessed November 8, 2010.

41. PICO and IAF are two of the four largest congregation-based community organizations (CBCOs). The other two are the Gamaliel Foundation and Direct Action Research and Training (DART). All the CBCO networks focus on training community organizers through a congregation-based structure. Heidi J. Swarts, *Organizing Urban America: Secular and Faith-based Progressive Movements* (Minneapolis: University of Minnesota Press, 2008), 4.

42. "Who Are We?" Industrial Areas Foundation, http://www.industrialareasfoundation.org/who.html, accessed November 8, 2010.

43. "What Do We Do?" Industrial Areas Foundation, http://www.industrialareasfoundation.org/what.html, accessed November 8, 2010.

44. Richard L. Wood, *Faith in Action: Religion, Race, and Democratic Organizing in America* (Chicago: University of Chicago Press, 2002), 73.

45. "PICO Values," PICO National Network, http://www.piconetwork.org/about?id=0003, accessed November 8, 2010.

46. "Continuum of Response to Social Problems," PICO National Network, http://www.piconetwork.org/congregations/resources?id=0026, accessed November 8, 2010.

47. "About PICO: The PICO Community Organizing Model," PICO National Network, http://www.piconetwork.org/about?id=0002, accessed November 8, 2010.

48. "Issues and Results: Housing Opportunities," PICO National Network, http://www.piconetwork.org/issues/housing, accessed November 8, 2010.

49. "All Aboard PICO's 'Recovery Express,'" PICO National Network, http://www.piconetwork.org/recoveryexpress, accessed November 8, 2010.

50. "Blight Removal and Reconstruction," Industrial Areas Foundation, http://www.industrialareasfoundation.org/initiatives.html, accessed November 8, 2010.

51. "Accomplishments and History," Interfaith Worker Justice, http://www.iwj.org/template/page.cfm?id=93, accessed November 8, 2010.

52. Nile Harper, *Urban Churches, Vital Signs: Beyond Charity Toward Justice* (Grand Rapids: Eerdmans, 1999), 26.

53. "Mission and Vision," Interfaith Worker Justice, http://iwj.org/template/page.cfm?id=92, accessed November 8, 2010.

Selected Bibliography
and Resources

Books and Articles

Homelessness

Abbarno, John M., ed. *The Ethics of Homelessness.* Amsterdam: Rodopi, 1999.

Amster, Randall. *Street People and the Contested Realms of Public Space.* New York: LFB Scholarly, 2004.

Arnold, K. R. *Homelessness, Citizenship, and Identity: The Uncanniness of Late Modernity.* Albany: State University of New York Press, 2004.

Bahr, Howard M. *Skid Row: An Introduction to Disaffiliation.* New York: Oxford University Press, 1973.

Barak, Gregg. *Gimme Shelter: A Social History of Homelessness in Contemporary America.* New York: Praeger, 1991.

Bogard, Cynthia J. *Seasons Such as These: How Homelessness Took Shape in America.* New York: Aldine De Gruyter, 2003.

Buck, Philip O., Paul A. Toro, and Melanie A. Ramos. "Media and Professional Interest in Homelessness over 30 Years (1974–2003)." *Analysis of Social Issues and Public Policy* 4, no. 1 (2004): 151–57.

Burt, Martha, Laudan Y. Aron, Edgar Lee, and Jesse Valente. *Helping America's Homeless: Emergency Shelter or Affordable Housing?* Washington, D.C.: Urban Institute Press, 2001.

Cloke, Paul, and Rebekah C. Widdowfield. "The Hidden and Emerging Spaces of Rural Homelessness." *Environmental and Planning A* 32 (2000): 77–90.

Del Casino, Vincent J., Jr., and Christine L. Jocoy. "Neoliberal Subjectivities, the 'New' Homelessness, and Struggles Over Spaces of/in the City." *Antipode* 40, no. 2 (2008): 192–99.

Depastino, Todd. *Citizen Hobo: How a Century of Homelessness Shaped America.* Chicago: University of Chicago Press, 2003.

Feldman, Leonard C. *Citizens Without Shelter: Homelessness, Democracy, and Political Exclusion*. Ithaca, N.Y.: Cornell University Press, 2004.

Fraser, Nancy. "Struggle Over Needs: Outline of a Socialist-Feminist Critical Theory of Late-Capitalist Political Culture." In *Women, Welfare, and the State*, edited by Londa Gordon, 199–225. Madison: University of Wisconsin Press, 1990.

Goodman, Lisa, Leonard Saxe, and Mary Harvey. "Homelessness as Psychological Trauma: Broadening Perspectives." *American Psychologist* 46, no. 11 (1991): 1219–25.

Hepworth, Mike. "Privacy, Security, and Respectability: The Ideal Victorian Home." In *Ideal Homes: Social Change and Domestic Life*, edited by Tony Chapman and Jenny Hockey, 17–29. New York: Routledge, 1999.

Hopper, Kim. *Reckoning with Homelessness*. Ithaca, N.Y.: Cornell University Press, 2003.

Johnson, Kelly S. *The Fear of Beggars: Stewardship and Poverty in Christian Ethics*. Grand Rapids: Eerdmans, 2007.

Karger, Howard. "The Home Ownership Myth." *Dollars & Sense: The Magazine of Economic Justice* 270 (Spring 2007): 13–19.

Kusmer, Kenneth L. *Down and Out, On the Road: The Homeless in American History*, New York: Oxford University Press, 2002.

Kyle, Ken. *Contextualizing Homelessness: Critical Theory, Homelessness, and Federal Policy Addressing the Homeless*. New York: Routledge, 2005.

Lee, Barrett A., Sue Hinze Jones, and David W. Lewis. "Public Beliefs About the Causes of Homelessness." *Social Forces* 69, no. 1 (1990): 253–65.

Lee, Barrett A., David W. Lewis, and Susan Hinze Jones. "Are the Homeless to Blame? A Test of Two Theories." *The Sociological Quarterly* 33, no. 4 (1992): 535–52.

Liebow, Elliot. *Tell Them Who I Am: The Lives of Homeless Women*. New York: Free, 1993.

Lyon-Callo, Vincent. *Inequality, Poverty, and Neoliberal Governance: Activist Ethnography in the Homeless Sheltering Industry*. Peterborough, Ont.: Broadview, 2004.

May, Elaine Tyler. *Homeward Bound: American Families in the Cold War Era*. New York: Basic, 1988.

Marvasti, Amir B. *Being Homeless: Textual and Narrative Constructions*. Lanham, Md.: Lexington, 2003.

Moch, Cheryl, ed. *Feels Like Home*. Chapel Hill: Algonquin Books of Chapel Hill, 1995.

Passaro, Joanne. *The Unequal Homeless: Men on the Streets, Women in Their Places*. New York: Routledge, 1996.

Ralston, Meredith L. *Nobody Wants to Hear Our Truth: Homeless Women and Theories of the Welfare State*. Westport, Conn.: Greenwood, 1996.

Rennebohm, Craig, with David Paul. *Souls in the Hands of a Tender God: Stories of the Search for Home and Healing on the Streets*. Boston: Beacon, 2008.

Rice, Douglas, and Barbara Said. "The Effects of the Federal Budget Squeeze on Low Income Housing Assistance." Center on Budget and Policy Priorities (February 1, 2007), http://www.cbpp.org/cms/?fa=view&id=1039, accessed November 9, 2010.

Rouner, Leroy S., ed. *The Longing for Home*. Notre Dame: University of Notre Dame Press, 1996.

Ruddick, Susan. "Heterotopias of the Homeless: Strategies and Tactics of Placemaking in Los Angeles." *Journal of Theory, Culture, and Politics* 3, no. 3 (1990): 184–201.

——. "From the Politics of Homelessness to the Politics of the Homeless." In *Local Places in the Age of the Global City*, edited by Roger Keil, Gerda R. Wekerle, and David V. J. Bell, 165–74. Montreal: Black Rose, 1996.

Shinn, Marybeth. "International Homelessness: Policy, Socio-Cultural, and Individual Perspectives." *Journal of Social Issues* 63, no. 3 (2007): 657–77.

Sibley, David. *Geographies of Exclusion: Society and Difference in the West*. New York: Routledge, 1995.

Timmer, Doug A., Stanley D. Eitzen, and Kathryn D. Talley. *Paths to Homelessness: Extreme Poverty and the Urban Housing Crisis*. Boulder: Westview, 1994.

Tompsett, Carolyn J., Paul A. Toro, Melissa Guzicki, Manuel Manrique, and Jigna Zatakia. "Homelessness in the United States: Assessing Changes in Prevalence and Public Opinion, 1993–2001." *American Journal of Community Psychology* 37, nos. 1/2 (2006): 47–61.

Toro, Paul A. "Toward an International Understanding of Homelessness." *Journal of Social Issues* 63, no. 3 (2007): 461–81.

——, and Carolyn J. Tompsett. "Homelessness in Europe and the United States: A Comparison of Prevalence and Public Opinion. *Journal of Social Issues* 63, no. 3 (2007): 505–24.

Vale, Lawrence J. *From the Puritans to the Projects: Public Housing and Public Neighbors*. Cambridge, Mass.: Harvard University Press, 2000.

Weinberg, Darin. *Of Others Inside: Insanity, Addiction, and Belonging in America*. Philadelphia: Temple University Press, 2005.

Wolch, Jennifer R. *The Shadow State: Government and Voluntary Sector in Transition*. New York: The Foundation Center, 1990.

Wright, James D., and Beth A. Rubin. "Is Homelessness a Housing Problem?" *Housing Policy Debate* 2, no. 3 (1997): 937–56.

Poverty and Oppression

Barndt, Joseph. *Understanding and Dismantling Racism: The Twenty-First Century Challenge to White America*. Minneapolis: Fortress Press, 2007.

Bobo, Kim. *Wage Theft in America: Why Millions of Working American Are Not Getting Paid—And What We Can Do About It*. New York: New Press, 2009.

Bounds, Elizabeth M., Pamela K. Brubaker, and Mary E. Hobgood. *Welfare Policy: Feminist Critiques*. Cleveland: Pilgrim, 1999.

Gans, Herbert J. *The War Against the Poor: The Underclass and Antipoverty Policy*. New York: Basic Books, 1995.

Johnson, Heather Beth. *The American Dream and the Power of Wealth: Choosing Schools and Inheriting Inequality in the Land of Opportunity*. New York: Routledge, 2006.

Reed, Adolph, Jr. "The Underclass as Myth and Symbol: The Poverty of Discourse About Poverty." *Radical America* 24 (1990): 21–40.

Thompson, Michael J. *Politics of Inequality: A Political History of the Idea of Economic Inequality in America.* New York: Columbia University Press, 2007.

Uchitelle, Louis. *The Disposable American: Layoffs and Their Consequences.* New York: Knopf, 2006.

Christian Theology and Ethics

Bouma-Prediger, Steven, and Brian J. Walsh. *Beyond Homelessness: Christian Faith in a Culture of Displacement.* Grand Rapids: Eerdmans, 2008.

Brock, Rita Nakashima, and Rebecca Ann Parker. *Saving Paradise: How Christianity Traded Love of This World for Crucifixion and Empire.* Boston: Beacon, 2008.

Gutiérrez, Gustavo. *A Theology of Liberation.* Trans. Sister Caridad Inda and John Eagleson. Rev. ed. Maryknoll, N.Y.: Orbis, 1988.

Koenig, John. *New Testament Hospitality: Partnership with Strangers as Promise and Mission.* Overtures to Biblical Theology. Minneapolis: Fortress Press, 1985.

King, Martin Luther, Jr. "The Strength to Love," in *A Testament of Hope: The Essential Writings of Martin Luther King, Jr.,* ed. James M. Washington, 491–517. San Francisco: HarperSanFrancisco, 1986.

Kroloff, Charles A. *When Elijah Knocks: A Religious Response to Homelessness.* West Orange, N.J.: Behrman House, 1992.

Niebuhr, Reinhold. *Moral Man and Immoral Society.* New York: Charles Scribner's Sons, 1960.

Newman, Elizabeth. *Untamed Hospitality: Welcoming God and Other Strangers: The Christian Practice of Everyday Life.* Grand Rapids: Brazos, 2007.

Pohl, Christine D. *Making Room: Recovering Hospitality as a Christian Tradition.* Grand Rapids: Eerdmans, 1999.

Russell, Letty M., Shannon J. Clarkson, and Kate M. Ott. *Just Hospitality: God's Welcome in a World of Difference.* Louisville: Westminster John Knox, 2009.

Smith, James K. A., and Henry Isaac Venema, eds. *The Hermeneutics of Charity: Interpretation, Selfhood, and Postmodern Faith.* Grand Rapids: Brazos, 2004.

Todd, George. "A Reformed Perspective on Faith-Based Initiatives: How Do We Apply Our Theology to Charitable Choice?" *Church & Society,* Presbyterian Church (U.S.A.) (May/June 2001): 76–80.

Wallis, Jim. *God's Politics: Why the Right Gets It Wrong and the Left Doesn't Get It.* San Francisco: HarperSanFrancisco, 2006.

West, Traci C. *Wounds of the Spirit: Black Women, Violence, and Resistance Ethics.* New York: New York University Press, 1999.

——. "Agenda for the Churches: Uprooting a National Policy of Morally Stigmatizing Poor Single Black Moms." In *Welfare Policy: Feminist Critiques,* edited by Elizabeth M. Bounds, Pamela K. Brubaker, and Mary E. Hobgood, 133–56. Cleveland: Pilgrim, 1999.

——. *Disruptive Christian Ethics: When Racism and Women's Lives Matter.* Louisville: Westminster John Knox, 2006.

———. "Gendered Legacies of Martin Luther King Jr.'s Leadership." *Theology Today* 65, no. 1 (April 2008): 41.

Community Organizing

Dreier, Peter. "Community Organizing for What? Progressive Politics and Movement Building in America." In *Transforming the City: Community Organizing and the Challenge of Political Change,* edited by Marion Orr, 218–51. Lawrence: University Press of Kansas, 2007.

Orr, Marion, ed. *Transforming the City: Community Organizing and the Challenge of Political Change.* Lawrence: University Press of Kansas, 2007.

Payne, Ruby K., Philip E. DeVol, and Terie Dreussi Smith. *Bridges Out of Poverty: Strategies for Professionals and Communities.* Highlands, Tex.: aha! Process, Inc., 2001.

Repo, Marjaleena. "Organising 'the Poor'—Against the Working Class." *Transformation* 1, no. 2 (March/April 1971): 4–15.

Shook, Jill Suzanne, ed. *Making Housing Happen: Faith-Based Affordable Housing Models.* St. Louis: Chalice, 2006.

Small, Stephen. "The Contours of Racialization: Structures, Representations, and Resistance in the United States." In *Race, Identity, and Citizenship: A Reader,* edited by Rodolfo D. Torres, Louis F. Mirón, and Jonathan Xavier Inda, 47–64. Hoboken, N.J.: Blackwell, 1999.

Tilly, Charles. *Social Movements 1768–2004.* Boulder: Paradigm, 2004.

Wood, Richard L. *Faith in Action: Religion, Race, and Democratic Organizing in America.* Chicago: University of Chicago Press, 2002.

Habitat for Humanity and Association of Gospel Rescue Missions

Baggett, Jerome P. *Habitat for Humanity: Building Private Homes, Building Public Religion.* Philadelphia: Temple University Press, 2001.

Burger, Delores T. *Women Who Changed the Heart of the City: The Untold Story of the City Rescue Mission Movement.* Grand Rapids: Kregel, 1997.

Fuller, Millard. *More Than Houses: How Habitat for Humanity Is Transforming Lives and Neighborhoods.* Nashville: Word, 2000.

———, with Diane Scott. *No More Shacks! The Daring Vision of Habitat for Humanity.* Waco: Word, 1986.

Gaillard, Frye. *If I Were a Carpenter: Twenty Years of Habitat for Humanity.* Winston-Salem: John F. Blair, 1996.

Habitat for Humanity, International. *Kingdom Building for the 21st Century: Voices from the Soul of Habitat for Humanity.* Americus, Ga.: Habitat for Humanity, 2006.

Leonard, Paul. *Music of a Thousand Hammers: Inside Habitat for Humanity.* New York: Continuum, 2006.

Reckford, Jonathan T. M. *Creating a Habitat for Humanity: No Hands but Yours.* Minneapolis: Fortress Press, 2007.

Youngs, Bettie B. *The House That Love Built: The Story of Millard & Linda Fuller Founders of Habitat for Humanity and the Fuller Center for Housing.* Charlottesville, Va.: Hampton Roads, 2007.

Web Sites

Corporation for Supportive Housing, www.csh.org

Department of Housing and Urban Development, www.hud.gov

Invisible People Blog, invisiblepeople.tv/blog

Joint Center for Housing Studies of Harvard University, www.jchs.harvard.edu

National Alliance to End Homelessness, www.endhomelessness.org

National Coalition for the Homeless, www.nationalhomeless.org

National Housing Institute, www.nhi.org/

National Law Center on Homelessness and Poverty, www.nlchp.org

National Low Income Housing Coalition, www.nlihc.org

The Urban Institute, www.urban.org/housing/index.cfm

(All sites accessed November 9, 2010.)

Congregation-Based Community Organizations

Direct Action Research and Training Center (DART), www.thedartcenter.org

Gamaliel Foundation, www.gamaliel.org

Industrial Areas Foundation (IAF), www.industrialareasfoundation.org

Interfaith Worker Justice (IWJ), www.iwj.org

Pacific Institute for Community Organizations (PICO), www.piconetwork.org

The Poor People's Economic Human Rights Campaign, old.economichumanrights.org

Sojourners, www.sojo.net

(All sites accessed November 9, 2010.)

Journals

Shelter Force: The Journal of Affordable Housing and Community Building, www.shelterforce.org

Housing Policy Debate, www.mi.vt.edu/publications/housing_policy_debate/hpd-index.html

(All sites accessed November 9, 2010.)

Index

addiction, 32–34, 37, 48–50, 58–59, 72–
74, 84–85, 107–11, 165n5, 165n13,
165n15
  as disease, 78–79
  as sin, 77–78
addiction-recovery program, 69, 71,
73–74, 80, 107–8, 111
advocacy, 7, 18, 22, 102–3, 122–25, 129,
131–32, 134–35, 139–40, 142–44
affordable and low-income housing, vii,
1–3, 5, 25, 27–28, 33, 37–42, 49, 53,
59, 62, 72, 76, 88, 102–4, 108, 110,
117–20, 127–30, 135–36, 139–41,
143, 156n82, 156n84, 166n33
agency, 8–9, 11, 13, 16–17, 20, 55, 74,
109, 112, 122
Alinsky, Saul, 141
American Dream, 2, 4, 43–44, 46, 53,
62–67, 77, 90, 92–93, 99, 126
anti-homeless laws, 58
Arnold, Kathleen, 45, 47
Association of Gospel Rescue Mission
(AGRM), 3, 5, 68–86, 105–12, 116–
18, 122, 165n7, 167n63, 167n64,
167–168n74, 168n75

Baggett, Jerome, 95, 116, 168n4
Bahr, Howard, 49, 152n19, 160n31
Baltimoreans United in Leadership
Development (BUILD), 145
Baron, David 139

Bobo, Kim, 145–46
Bogardin, Cynthia, 52
Bouma-Prediger, Steven, 49
Brock, Rita Nakashima, 124, 174n2
Brosch, Eric, 58
Burden, Virginia, 98
Burger, Stephen, 72–73, 76, 80, 108,
167n63
Burt, Jason and Casey, 98
Burt, Martha, 31, 34

capitalism, 57, 59, 61, 64, 117–18, 170n53
Carter, Jimmy, 89, 96
Center for Budget and Policy Priorities,
28, 41
charity, 2, 4–5, 7, 17, 22, 24, 55, 57, 69,
73, 85–86, 96, 99, 104, 117, 123,
125–27, 129, 138, 147
children, 11, 30–33, 35–37, 39–42, 44,
49, 52, 57, 63, 72, 74–75, 87, 90–98,
111, 113, 139, 156n82
Christie, Paul, 132
church communities and congregations,
2–3, 14, 18, 22, 41–42, 66, 85,
88, 102–4, 120–24, 128–29, 132,
136–48, 150n2
Churches United for the Homeless, 139
citizens and citizenship, 15, 19, 43–44,
47, 56, 60, 65–66, 93, 114
class, 2, 10–15, 20, 25, 34, 44, 47, 50–51,
56–59, 62–66, 75, 85, 92, 111–16,

tax credits, deductions, and subsidies, 28–29, 40–41, 46, 60, 65, 130
tent city, 1, 133–34, 162n63
theology of the hammer, 97, 102
Tilly, Charles, 128
Timmer, Doug, 50

U.S. Conference of Mayors, 32
undeserving poor, 4, 13, 27, 49, 52, 57–58, 65, 108–13, 115–16, 121
Urban Institute, 31, 33–34, 182
urban renewal, 26–27, 37–38, 49

Verret, Jeremy, 77
veterans, 26, 32, 37, 41, 60
victimization, 1, 9, 15–17, 20, 52–56, 60, 67, 86, 106, 109, 119, 122, 136
violence, 9, 12, 14–15, 120, 123, 131, 136, 151n10

Walsh, Brian J., 49
welfare, 23, 29, 33, 35–36, 47, 49, 51, 59–61, 90, 111, 118–19
West, Traci, 3–4, 7, 9, 12, 15–17, 105–6, 113, 119, 121, 149n5
Wolch, Jennifer, 61, 119
women, 9–12, 15–16, 24, 32, 36–37, 45, 47, 52–56, 70, 73–74, 78–79, 83–84, 106–7, 109, 111–13, 135, 137, 139, 151n10, 166n30
Wood, Richard, 142
working-class people, 2, 112, 115, 128, 131, 134

youth, 30, 32, 37, 39, 53, 69, 113, 117, 120, 135, 137, 139, 163n75, 172n8

CPSIA information can be obtained
at www.ICGtesting.com
Printed in the USA
JSHW060825031222
34260JS00008BA/76